Counseling
and the
Search for Meaning

RESOURCES FOR
CHRISTIAN COUNSELING

RESOURCES FOR CHRISTIAN COUNSELING

(Other volumes forthcoming)

VOLUME NINE

Counseling and the Search for Meaning

PAUL R. WELTER, Ed.D.

RESOURCES FOR CHRISTIAN COUNSELING

—— General Editor ——

Gary R. Collins, Ph.D.

WORD BOOKS
PUBLISHER
WACO, TEXAS
A DIVISION OF
WORD, INCORPORATED

Permission to reprint from the following sources is gratefully acknowledged:
The Three Boxes of Life by Richard N. Bolles, © 1978, 1981. Published by Ten Speed Press. The Unheard Cry for Meaning © 1978 by Viktor E. Frankl. Published by Simon & Schuster, Inc. Man's Search for Meaning © 1962 by Viktor Frankl. Published by Beacon Press. "New Ways to Talk About Children" from Varsity Educator, © 1986. Published by SRI Perceiver Academies, Inc. "Sin" from Prayers © 1963 by Michel Quoist. Published by Sheed & Ward, 115 E. Armour Blvd., Kansas City, Mo. Connecting with a Friend © 1985 by Paul Welter. Published by Tyndale House Publishers, Inc.

Scripture quotations in this publication identified NIV are from the New International Version of the Bible, copyright © 1983 by the New York International Bible Society. Used by permission of Zondervan Bible Publishers. Scripture quotations identified TEV are from the Good News Bible, the Bible in Today's English Version, © 1966, 1971, 1976 American Bible Society.

An Institute of Logotherapy Book

Library of Congress Cataloging-in-Publication Data

Welter, Paul, 1928–
    Counseling and the search for meaning.

    (Resources for Christian counseling ; v. 9)
    Includes index.
    1. Pastoral counseling.   2. Counseling.
I. Title.   II. Series.
BV4012.2.W423   1987   253.5   87-13562
ISBN 0-8499-0584-2

7 8 9 8 FG 9 8 7 6 5 4 3 2 1

CONTENTS

EDITOR'S PREFACE

I HAVE A FRIEND who is twenty-one years old. He is a brilliant young man whose test scores place him in the top 1 percent of the college-age population. If you could meet him, you would be impressed immediately by his social charm, his quick wit, and his ability to talk comfortably and knowledgeably on a variety of topics.

But he just flunked out of college.

My friend complained that the main reason for this failure was that he couldn't get motivated. "I don't know where I am going in life," he said. "My spiritual life is blah, my classes were boring, and my future is a big, vague question mark. Why knock myself out in college when my life doesn't have any meaning?"

When I first assembled a list of possible authors to write these Resources for Christian Counseling books, I thought of Dr. Paul Welter. He has established himself as an insightful Christian counselor and I had been impressed by his earlier

9

books, especially *How to Help a Friend* (published by Tyndale House). I was surprised, however, when he proposed writing a book on counseling people, like my young friend, whose lives are meaningless. I wasn't sure this was a major issue, especially for pastoral counselors, and Paul Welter had to convince me.

I am glad he did. As the author shows in the following pages, a sense of meaninglessness permeates many lives, including the lives of people who are active members of local churches. At times, probably all of us feel that life has no purpose; no wonder that this leads to discouragement, emptiness, and the drifting that currently characterizes my young college-age friend.

For a number of years Viktor Frankl's *Man's Search for Meaning* was required reading for all incoming freshmen at a Christian liberal arts college where I taught. The book was written by a non-Christian whose conclusions arose partially from his experiences in a Nazi death camp, but our students were profoundly impressed. Many of them were starting college with no clear direction in life, and they were able to understand a man who wrote about the problem of meaninglessness.

Frankl's work and counseling methods are presented with clarity in the following pages, but Paul Welter does more than summarize a secular approach to counseling. Drawing from his rich clinical experience and pointing frequently to the pages of Scripture, he offers practical guidance for all of us who experience meaninglessness or who counsel with those—including Christians—whose lives seem to be empty.

A discussion of this common problem fits well into the Resources for Christian Counseling series. Each of these books is intended to deal with some topic that is likely to come up in your counseling. Written by counseling experts, each of whom has a strong Christian commitment and practical counseling experience, these volumes are intended to be examples of accurate psychology and careful use of Scripture. Each is intended to have a clear evangelical perspective, a strong practical orientation, careful documentation, and freedom from the sweeping statements and undocumented rhetoric that sometimes characterize books in the counseling field. Our goal is to provide books that are clearly written, practical, up-to-date overviews of the issues faced by contemporary Christian counselors. All of the Resources for Christian Counseling books have similar bindings and together they will comprise a complete encyclopedia of Christian counseling.

Many centuries ago, the author of another book wrote that life for many people is filled with meaninglessness. "Meaningless! Meaningless!" wrote wise King Solomon in the beginning of his book. "Utterly meaningless! Everything is meaningless" (Eccles. 1:2 NIV). This was the same man who wrote that "there is nothing new under the sun" (Eccles. 1:9 NIV). The meaninglessness that exists in so many lives today has been around for centuries.

The ultimate answer to meaninglessness is also centuries-old. Speaking of his followers, Jesus announced, "I have come that they may have life, and have it to the full" (John 10:10b NIV). The ultimate answer to meaninglessness is found in Christ. This book will help you bring counselees to this realization.

I suspect you will appreciate Paul Welter's insights, thoughtful examples, theory mixed with practical directions, and biblical conclusions—all presented in short, easy-to-digest chapters. Some day, I hope my young college drop-out friend will find the meaning that is written about in the stimulating pages that follow. Perhaps someone who reads this book will be his counselor.

Gary R. Collins, Ph.D.
Kildeer, Illinois

ACKNOWLEDGMENTS

I AM INDEBTED to Dr. Viktor Frankl for the clarity and usefulness of his writings. Dr. James Yoder has been my personal mentor in logotherapy. Colleagues and students at Kearney State College have also advanced my thinking in the area. My clients have taught me much about the search for meaning by their courageous search for meaning and by suffering bravely endured. Their names have been changed and their situations disguised to assure their anonymity.

I appreciate the light touch and substantive help of Gary Collins. Readers of major portions of this manuscript include Bill Coleman, the Rev. Dennis Doke, Mrs. Grace Kannady, and Dr. James Yoder. I value their wisdom. Lillian, my wife, has been my partner on this venture by working on the word processor, by encouragement, and by giving useful suggestions.

INTRODUCTION

THIS BOOK FLOWS out of my own counseling experiences. For more than twenty-five years I have spent the bulk of my time either counseling or training others to counsel. During those years, I found that in the thousands of counseling sessions I have held, the subject of meaning—or the lack of it—was often at the center. It occurred so often, in fact, that about four years ago I began a Self-Directed Learning Project (SDLP) which was entitled "Counseling Those Who Lack Meaning." The SDLP resources and strategies involved considerable reading on the subject, attending conferences and training events on logotherapy, talking with many people about the topic, enlarging my awareness of this component in my counseling, and taking a systematic look at my own meaning in life. In addition, for the past two years I have taught a college seminar course called "Counseling Those Who Lack Meaning," and I have led a number of workshops for pastors on that topic.

Usually, I will have two or three SDLPs going at any given time. They have added an important meaning dimension to my life over the years. I have also asked my students to do SDLPs as a part of their classwork. They like to know that I practice what I teach. The SDLP model which I presently teach to my students and which I have used myself for the last five years is from *The Modern Practice of Adult Education: From Pedagogy to Andragogy* by Malcolm Knowles.[1] The final step in his SDLP model is to gather and write one's findings. This book is that step, the culmination of my years of research, learning, and experience.

You probably noticed that the table of contents indicated a broad coverage of counseling concerns. I want to respond to two possible questions concerning this wide spectrum. The first question is, "Are there not other books, and even some in this Resources for Christian Counseling series, that speak to some of these problems?" The answer is yes. The rationale for their inclusion here is that they are treated in terms of their relationship to the search for meaning. This does not relieve us of the responsibility to study other resources which treat these problems from different perspectives.

A second question that may be asked is, "Does the treatment of so many counseling problems limit the depth of each treatment?" My response is that the common thread of counseling for meaning will serve to connect and deepen the treatment of these problems. Five clients may present five different tapestry designs, but on the reverse side of each design there is a common pattern of despair, futility, and meaninglessness. I am not suggesting that all counseling problems have their roots here, but many symptoms are complicated by a sense of meaninglessness, and several have this as their chief source.

Once you have read this book, I hope it will become a valuable tool in your counseling ministry. When a client causes you to suspect the presence of meaninglessness, you can quickly scan the table of contents of this book. Then you can choose those relevant chapters which will enable you to effectively counsel that client.

PART ONE

RECOGNIZING AND UNDERSTANDING THE PROBLEM

IT WAS A COLD wintry Sunday. I had gone downtown to mail a letter and had parked across from the post office. Before getting out of the car, I looked down the almost deserted street and saw patches of snow here and there. Then I saw something that kept me in the car. There was a man, rather stooped, slowly walking with the aid of a cane. He appeared to be close to eighty years old. I watched him as he stopped at a street corner about half a block from where I was parked and looked intently at a small patch of snow by a light pole. Then he glanced around, apparently to make sure no one was watching. From my hidden vantage point, I saw him step forward and carefully place one foot in the snow. He stepped back, looked at the footprint, then repeated the action with the other foot. He then stepped back several steps, surveyed the area again for observers, looked thoughtfully at the two footprints, and walked on.

I sat in my car for a long time, thinking about this scene I had witnessed. It seemed to me that the creation of the footprints was a metaphor for this man's life and for all our lives. We would like to know that our imprint has made some difference, that our lives are significant. In other words, we seek meaning.

Meaning, as used here, refers to the significance we attach to our existence. The lack of such meaning can be devastating. Meaninglessness is often the root of depression, violence, felt inadequacy, and other kinds of suffering. Usually the client is not aware of this real source of the malady because meaninglessness is, by definition, a vacuum. It is difficult to be aware of what is not visible. We cannot see the wind, but its effects are obvious. In the same way, a counselor will sometimes focus on the effect rather than the source.

The three chapters that follow are aimed at helping counselors enlarge their awareness of the symptoms that indicate meaninglessness and underlying despair.

CHAPTER ONE

CHASING THE WIND

"I HAVE SEEN all the things that are done under the sun; all of them are meaningless, a chasing after the wind" (Eccl. 1:14 NIV). Solomon frequently used the metaphor of chasing the wind to describe his own search for meaning as recorded in the Book of Ecclesiastes.

Picture a man on a hill dashing madly first one direction, then the other in his futile attempt to keep up with the ever-changing gusts of wind. At first the experience appears to be invigorating. There is freshness and joy in his face, and a lightness in his step. But the day wears on and the sun beats down. His frenzied pace slows as the meadow is transformed into a swamp. He moves more slowly, but still with determination.

17

Soon, he just "goes through the motions" as he struggles for enough energy to keep going. Suddenly, the man collapses, buries his face in his hands, and cries—or wants to. But he cannot find rest or peace, so he gets up slowly, and with great effort continues his aimless task. The sadness in this picture is that the wind chaser has no clear purpose and, therefore, little hope. In Ecclesiastes, Solomon described some of the elusive goals he pursued to satisfy his emptiness.

PLEASURES ARE MEANINGLESS

"I thought in my heart, 'Come now, I will test you with pleasure to find out what is good.' But that also proved to be meaningless" (Eccl. 2:1 NIV). Like moths circling closer and closer to the flame, pleasure-seekers desire the warmth of happiness. Both efforts can be self-destructive. Their motto can be aptly described by the message of bumper stickers I have seen on some recreational vehicles, "We're having a good time, aren't we?"

This young king tried all the pleasures money could buy. He engaged in endless frivolity. He built expansive and expensive buildings to beautify his kingdom. He tried to find happiness in wine, women, and song. As a matter of fact, Solomon had a harem. He had not only tasted the pleasures of sex—he had satiated himself with sexual delights: " . . . I had all the women a man could want" (Eccl. 2:8 TEV). But his practice of using women backfired. Mignon Eisenberg has noted that "Sex without love is nothing but masturbation on another person, resulting in lowered self-esteem."[1] Actually, Solomon not only felt devalued himself, he also devalued others, " . . . I found one man in a thousand that I could respect, but not one woman" (Eccl. 7:28).

The reason that pleasure did not satisfy him is that the emptiness was within himself. And we, feeling the same emptiness, look to things or to others to fill it. People go to counselors because they are dissatisfied with their spouses, but as Rollo May has noted, " . . . they do not talk long before they make it clear that they expect the marriage partner . . . to fill some lack, some vacancy within themselves; and they are anxious and angry because he or she doesn't."[2]

WORK IS MEANINGLESS

When work becomes toil, it is a curse. "So I hated life, because the work that is done under the sun was grievous to me. All of it is meaningless, a chasing after the wind" (Eccl. 2:17). Such toil may be caused by a long and tense commute, wearisome physical labor, the performance of repetitively monotonous tasks, or the constant need for immediate responses to an ever increasing stack of "urgent" paper work. And even those who love their jobs have nothing of value to show for their labors. More often, the "rewards" come in the form of ulcers, stress, and nervous disorders.

SUCCESS IS MEANINGLESS

Solomon went the full length of the money-sex-power route. He amassed personal and public fortunes of silver and gold and he "became greater by far than anyone in Jerusalem before me" (Eccl. 2:9 NIV).

A minister had everything he had always wanted—a very large church, one that needed and used his gifts well, and a secure and prominent place in his denomination. If he could have painted a work setting and walked into it, this would be it. He had worked hard to get where he was, and he had reached the pinnacle of success in his community. Yet, he was suffering from anxiety attacks, he regularly took tranquilizers to help him make it through the worship service, and he went through the week on cruise control.

Solomon, too, was a success. He had all that money could buy. "Yet when I surveyed all that my hands had done and what I had toiled to achieve, everything was meaningless, a chasing after the wind; nothing was gained under the sun" (Eccl. 2:11 NIV).

WISDOM IS MEANINGLESS

Many would agree that pleasures are empty, work can gradually turn into toil, and success is not what it's cracked up to be. But surely wisdom cannot turn sour! Just as Solomon had climbed the mountain in pleasures, work, and success, he also was at the top in wisdom. And from this vantage point he gave his view: "I said in my heart, 'This, too, is meaningless.' For the wise man, like the fool, will not be long remembered; in days to come both will be forgotten. Like the fool, the wise man too must die!" (Eccl. 2:15–16).

WEARY, PURPOSELESS REPETITION

Hearing the same phrases again and again is tiresome. Is there no end? The wisdom of Ecclesiastes is not only that it accurately describes for its readers the state of meaninglessness, but also that it actually *evokes* within the readers the emotions of one who is caught in such despair.

The reason I led you on this brief, weary trip through Ecclesiastes is simple. If we can feel some of the futility and despair of Solomon, we can perhaps better sense the futility and despair of the client who is struggling with his or her own lack of meaning in life.

CHAPTER TWO

THE NATURE OF MEANINGLESSNESS

To UNDERSTAND THE nature of meaninglessness, it is necessary for us to examine its specific symptoms, prevalence, demographics, and impact.

SPECIFIC SYMPTOMS

In addition to being aware of the characteristics discussed in Ecclesiastes as highlighted in the last chapter, we as counselors need to be alert for other symptoms as we observe and listen to a client.

Boredom

Sidney Jourard has discussed the death and rebirth cycle that many people experience throughout their lives. A part of the detaching and dying process is the fading of fascination with life. He says fascination may be observed in healthy children before they have been "turned off." "The 'turning off' begins with the experience of despair, boredom, or meaninglessness as one continues his habitual way of life—acting in one's roles, doing one's work, being one's public self."[1] Jourard emphasizes that we must be willing to let the fascination go and "to let the process unfold rather than shut it off."[2] The old has to go before the new will come. Later in this book we will deal with the rediscovery of meaning. It is enough for now to note that the loss of fascination with life is a telling symptom of meaninglessness.

Viktor Frankl noted that the existential vacuum (the inner emptiness which is the result of a lack of meaning) can lead to both boredom and anxiety: "Now we can understand Schopenhauer when he said that mankind was apparently doomed to vacillate eternally between the two extremes of distress and boredom."[3] The boredom caused by the humdrum of an empty life can propel us on a frenzied search— "chasing the wind"—that leaves us full of distress, and very tired. Then we move back across the territory of meaninglessness to the other border of boredom to rest and fret for awhile until we regain energy for another commute.

Anxiety

Existential anxiety is a part of the human condition. Most of us admit to uneasiness and a vague fear, because of the choices, little and big, which we must make each day. When I was a boy on a Kansas farm, I would sometimes run across a stream, stepping from rock to rock. Once I committed myself to this venture, I had to keep running and choosing, or I would fall in. Life is like that.

For some, those who are panicked because of a lack of purpose in their lives, the anxiety is worse because panic has blurred their vision and the choices are unclear. Most clients (and counselors) display some anxiety, so it is up to the counselor by careful observation and questioning to determine if meaninglessness is contributing to the state of anxiety, or if the anxiety can be explained by other factors. One of the chapters which follows, "Socratic Questioning," may be useful in helping you make this diagnosis.

The Thirst for Something More

There is a saying among logotherapists (counselors who see meaning as the primary motivator in life) that those who are struggling with existential frustration, have everything, but are satisfied with nothing. Sigmund Freud said that pleasure motivates people. Alfred Adler opted for the power principle. Everyone wants a "place"—social power. Yet Elisabeth Lukas argued that today's youth have "discredited" both Freud and Adler because youth have the privileges of sexuality and power, but have not thereby become happy.[4] Their thirst continues because their pleasure and power have no lasting meaning.

Excessive Dependence

Some have suffered an early wounding in their growing-up families that has left them enmeshed with their parents and, to some extent, undifferentiated from them. The reality behind the term "terrible twos" is that it is about that age when little children are heavily involved in learning where their parents leave off and they begin. They are in the process of differentiating themselves from their parents. There are a considerable number of adults who are still stuck in that process. Sometimes fear and guilt have been contributors to their continuing dependence on their parents.

One of the tragedies of this enmeshed state is that a thirty-five-year-old may not know how to discover meaning on his own. He is consumed with seeking his parents' help, and resenting their "interference." He will seek friends and a spouse on whom he can be dependent. The individual search for meaning will be terrifying.

Irresponsibility

A client whose life is characterized by a lack of responsibility may be suffering from meaninglessness. Responsible people usually have a clear direction in their lives. Meaning is a strong motivator to becoming responsible. This is one reason why an increased sense of responsibility usually occurs in the life of a newly converted person.

Lack of Goals

Counseling with those who lack meaning in life is challenging. The clients' empty lives lack the internal consistency and strength that permit response and movement. The inner emptiness results in existential frustration, an emotional state characterized by a deep sense of futility. Clients are left with no clear purpose. Even if they have some goals, they no longer think these are attainable because hope is gone.

The "Mass Neurotic Triad"

Viktor Frankl has referred to depression, addiction, and aggression as the "mass neurotic triad."[5] The despair of meaninglessness is a major factor in each of these. Therefore, these three major disorders may often be viewed as symptomatic of a lack of purpose in life. These disorders will be discussed more fully in later chapters.

PREVALENCE

If the "mass neurotic triad"—depression, addiction, and aggression—is spawned by a sense of meaninglessness, then meaninglessness is indeed a pervasive condition in our society. Never have we had more depressed, addicted, and violent people than we have today. Estimates vary somewhat as to the prevalence of these disorders, but all agree that the magnitude of each is very large. A Public Health Service source says that "from 4 to 10 percent of the American public now suffers from an identifiable depressive disorder."[6] The same source gives an even more startling estimate: "Over the course of a lifetime, perhaps 25 percent of the population will experience a major depressive episode."[7] If this will be the experience of one in every four people, then can depression be considered abnormal, or even unusual?

In terms of addiction, one source estimates that over ten million Americans are alcoholics.[8] In fact, the leading cause of death among youth from the ages of sixteen to twenty-four is alcohol-related motor vehicle accidents.[9] Also, estimates indicate that twenty-three million Americans over twelve years of age have at one time or another used illegal drugs.[10] In 1985, arrests for drug abuse violations rose 23 percent above the 1981 level.[11]

And aggression? One of every four homes was touched by crime in 1985.[12] And much of the violence is between family and friends. Statistics show that victims and assailants know each other in about one-third of all violent crimes.[13]

These statistics show that the mass neurotic triad is indeed epidemic in scope. Millions of despairing people are retreating from life through the avenue of depression, reaching for excitement or numbness through addiction, and seeking power in their weakness by turning violent. And many depressed and/or anxious people turn aggressively and violently on themselves. Between the years 1958 and 1982, some 587,821 people in the United States alone ended their lives by self-inflicted injuries, an average of about 23,500 per year.[14] These were the reported suicides. The National Institute of Health has estimated the actual suicide rate in this country to be about 75,000 per year, a figure more than triple the number of reported suicides.[15] More women attempt suicide, but more men succeed. In fact, suicide is the second leading cause of death (after automobile accidents) in males between twenty-five and forty-five.[16] We obviously live in a critical age.

Paul Tillich concluded that "the anxiety which determines our period is the anxiety of doubt and meaninglessness."[17] A contemporary study of individualism and isolation in American life and their effect on the decline of meaning is reported in *Habits of the Heart*: "The erosion of meaning and coherence in our lives is not something Americans desire."[18] The authors went on to say that most of the people they talked to in their research project had a great yearning for " . . . the idealized small town . . . a yearning for just such meaning and coherence."[19] Viktor Frankl has noted that its prevalence extends beyond the United States. "Just consider the worldwide emergence and persistence of the feeling of meaninglessness," he says.[20] The evidences are compelling that meaninglessness is a widespread epidemic.

DEMOGRAPHIC FACTORS

Age

There has been a marked increase in teen suicide and in suicide among the elderly the past few years. You have heard their voices, and they sound remarkably alike. Even their words are the same: "I no longer have anything to live for. I just want to die." Suicide is the most crisp statement possible to express one's feelings of meaninglessness.

I've had counseling sessions with teens who don't see any reason to live, middle-aged people for whom the fascination with life has dimmed, and senior citizens who ask, "Why can't I just die?" Studies show that people are generally more likely to consider suicide during *transition* times in their lives— adolescence, mid-life, and retirement. And judging from my discussions with other counselors, this phenomenon appears to be quite widespread.

Economic Level

Clinically, one cannot establish a solid relationship between meaninglessness and economic level. It stands to reason that more people at mid- and high-salary ranges are able to seek counseling for this problem. Those with low income levels, on the other hand, usually cannot afford to pay for counseling, and are therefore less inclined to seek it.

There are other evidences, however, that affluence and the feeling of meaninglessness are indeed related. It seems that in affluent societies we have more leisure time but an apparent lack of meaningful activities to occupy that time. "All this adds up to the obvious conclusion that to the degree that man is spared want and tension he loses the capacity to endure them."[21]

Occupation

If we use high suicide rates as an indicator of meaninglessness, it appears that human service and health professionals are prime candidates to suffer from a lack of meaning. Physicians, especially psychiatrists, have a very high suicide rate. One researcher points out, "The general pattern is that suicide rates are highest in the most and least prestigious occupations and lowest in the intermediate occupations."[22]

IMPACT

According to the above evidences, the influence of a lack of meaning in life is very large. Meaninglessness is linked at one end of the scale to aggression and violence, and on the other to depression, immobilization, and passivity. Somewhere in between the violent and the depressed there are many others who can function at least marginally at home and at work, but they go about life with a kind of quiet desperation because the meaning of their lives is unclear to them. In addition to these emotional costs, the financial costs for medication, hospitalization, and treatment are in the billions of dollars.

But perhaps the greatest impact of all is on the children who are the burden bearers of this legacy of meaninglessness and despair.

CHAPTER THREE

THE CAUSES AND DYNAMICS
OF MEANINGLESSNESS

IN OUR SOCIETY people possess more than they ever have before, and still the epidemic of meaninglessness continues to spread. What are those factors which contribute to the lack of meaning in people's lives?

CAUSES OF MEANINGLESSNESS

Choosing Money over Meaning

The Cooperative Institutional Research Program Freshman Survey is our country's largest study of higher education. Over a quarter of a million students participate in the survey annually, and significant trends have been discovered using a number of variables over the years. Two of those trends are relevant here.

In one of the questions, students were asked to identify their goals in life. In 1967, about 83 percent chose the answer "developing a meaningful life." In 1984, this answer was chosen by only 47 percent. In contrast, about 43 percent of those surveyed in 1967 chose the goal "being very well-off financially." Since then, there has been a rather steady increase in college freshmen choosing that goal. In 1984, 71 percent chose it as their main goal in life.

The *Educational Record,* which reported the study, noted that "this material focus may reflect a major realignment of values on the college campus."[1] The explicit values of college freshmen are likely to mirror the implicit values of their parents. Therefore, the value shift from meaning to money reported in this freshman survey is probably widespread. The impact which this trend has on one's self-esteem is obvious since only a small percentage of the population can be considered "well-off financially."

Lack of Purpose

Joseph Fabry reported an interesting observation made by the chief of the psychiatric clinic at the Berkeley campus of the University of California during the 1960s. At the time of the free-speech demonstrations, clinic admissions dropped to almost zero. When the demonstrations were over, clinic admissions increased again. "Here is support for the thesis that mental health depends on having a meaning to fulfill, an ideal to strive for," Fabry said.[2] When we have a cause to which we devote our time and energy, we often "forget" about our ailments. This characteristic is also apparent in children. A child may fall down and skin his knee, but when the fun starts again the pain vanishes.

Affluence

It is not only the choice of money over meaning that contributes to meaninglessness. It is also the actual lifestyle of affluence. When we live with little money, then survival has great meaning. When we live in affluence, however, we lack that motivation which covered our emptiness. Now, our lack of meaning is clearly revealed. In addition, we have an uneasy conscience because we see the poor of the world on television, and we are not helping them.

The Specter of Nuclear Annihilation

It is the view of some opponents of nuclear proliferation that we have been "born into a coffin." Such a vision renders life-as-usual to be without meaning. This view has particularly affected the nation's youth, who have the most years to lose in the event of a nuclear war or accident. It also increases the frenzied activity of the hedonistic principle, "Eat, drink, and be merry, for tomorrow we die."

The Pursuit of Happiness

Our Declaration of Independence gives us the right to chase happiness. "Pursuit" is an accurate term because we cannot catch happiness. In fact, striving for hedonistic values is usually counter-productive and is sometimes destructive. This is true even in family relationships, which offer not only great happiness, but also terribly hard work and, at times, great suffering.

The "Demise" of Sin

Karl Menninger asked the question in the title of his book *Whatever Became of Sin?*[3] A theologian would be expected to ask that question, but should a psychiatrist? Now another psychiatrist, M. Scott Peck, is asking the same question. The thesis of his book *People of the Lie* is " . . . that the phenomenon of evil can and should be subjected to scientific scrutiny."[4] We still worry about psychological problems more than sin. But this loss of focus on sin has placed us in a predicament. If sin is recognized as a cause of meaninglessness, then there is hope because the remedy for sin is found in the cross of Christ. But if the power of sin is not recognized, then there is "no way out."

The Loss of a Sense of Gratitude

Paul Tournier has noted that we looked with wonder on the marvelous adventures of our growing-up days.[5] However, Tournier says, our children do not feel this wonder. "But let us not be mistaken, this generation basically is seeking a gift which ours has not been able to provide: a valid purpose for life."[6] He goes on to say that this is a result of their loss of a sense of gratitude. Our sense of gratitude is important because it places us in the right relationship to God. We experience meaning in life as we thank God.

DYNAMICS OF MEANINGLESSNESS

Traditional medicine has ministered to the body. Psychology has been useful in helping us understand the human mind. Frankl, trained both in medicine and psychology, has gone beyond them to emphasize, as a psychiatrist, the spiritual dimension of humankind. It is from our spiritual nature that the "will to meaning" springs. Logotherapy holds that " . . . the striving to find a meaning in one's life is the primary motivational force in man."[7] If this is true, it would explain why the inability to find meaning produces such great suffering.

Jean-Paul Sartre taught that people invent their own meaning.[8] Frankl takes the point of view that we detect or discover our meaning, rather than invent it.[9] This point of view has immense implications for counselors. It implies that meaning does exist in life, and that the counselor should be an authentic part of the search for that meaning. The stakes are high in that quest. If the search is successful, the client will experience a sense of usefulness and joy. If the search is a failure, the client may encounter one or more of several negative consequences.

Compensation

If people do not find meaning in their lives they are "stuck" in an existential vacuum. Since their will to have meaning is frustrated, they may compensate by a will to have pleasure or a will to have power. Many modern films and television offerings deal primarily with impersonal sex and needless violence, an evidence of the above compensation.

Frankl has discussed the "Sunday neurosis" which comes when the week's activities are completed and people have a little time to think of the emptiness of their lives.[10] This "sickness" contributes to alcoholism, juvenile delinquency, and other societal dilemmas.

Lack of Responsibility

Logotherapy has a categorical imperative: "Live as if you were living already for the second time and as if you had acted the first time as wrongly as you are about to act now!"[11] This imperative emphasizes the importance of our choices, and the moral nature of choice. It also suggests that if we do not think seriously about life, we will make wrong choices, choices which will result in an empty life.

Looking for Solutions Instead of Taking Action

We are always looking for solutions to the problems of life. Clients come to counselors for answers to their problems. But the cure for meaninglessness is not an answer. It is a choice followed by an action. An existential problem yields only to an existential solution.

Neuroses

Elisabeth Lukas has reported that "worldwide research has shown that 20 percent of all cases of psychological illnesses are caused not by childhood traumas and past conflicts but by an existential frustration and value conflict."[12] These illnesses are referred to by logotherapists as "noogenic neuroses," or mental illness caused by the stifling of the noetic (spiritual) dimension.

Lukas also noted that even in the 80 percent of psychological illnesses not necessarily caused by existential frustration, there exists "potential links" with existential frustration. Therefore, counselors are needed who can address the inner frustration brought about by an existential vacuum. Frankl has made an important distinction here. The concern over the "worthwhileness of life is a *spiritual distress* but by no means a *mental disease*."[13] He noted that making a misdiagnosis here "motivates a doctor to bury his patient's existential despair under a heap of tranquilizing drugs."[14] The counselor needs to avoid this mistake and be clear in diagnosing "spiritual distress" accurately.

PART TWO

SPECIFIC COUNSELING
APPROACHES AND METHODS

ONE OF THE EXCITING aspects of the Resources for Christian Counseling Series (RCC) is that the books are arranged by problem, not subject. The difference is a simple but profound one. Let's say, for instance, that I am flipping through a vocational school catalog and notice that one of the subjects offered is auto mechanics. At the time I might think it's a worthwhile subject but still have no interest in taking the course. However, if I'm driving on a rural Nebraska road and my car makes a few funny noises under the hood, lurches, and then suddenly comes to a stop miles from any help, I have a drastic change in my point of view. Suddenly my car's engine has become a problem instead of a subject for me, and I'm intensely motivated. Malcolm Knowles, a leading adult educator, says that the primary deficit in adult education today is that we arrange college courses, workshops, and books by subjects instead of problems.[1] We may yawn at subjects but we don't yawn at problems. So this series has a format that is motivating.

Taking this cue from Malcolm Knowles and from the RCC series, I have arranged part two of this book by problems, whenever possible. About half the chapter titles in this part of the book clearly indicate the problem, titles such as "Intervention with Cancer Patients," "Counseling the Depressed Person for Meaning," and "Violence and Meaning." Although the rest of the chapter titles indicate a subject—such as "Socratic Questioning," "Paradoxical Intention," and "Dereflection"—the approach in each chapter is to show how these methods can be used to tackle problems.

CHAPTER FOUR

LOVE AND MEANING

THERE ARE TWO things that give meaning to life: tasks and relationships. Jesus left us with a last commandment concerning a task when he said, "Go then, to all peoples everywhere and make them my disciples . . . " (Matt. 28:19 TEV). He also gave us a first commandment concerning relationships: "Love the Lord your God . . . " (Mark 12:30 TEV).

The whole concept of Christianity is relational—our relationships with God, with Christ, with each other. Even the mission of sharing the gospel is a loving relational task. Meaning in life comes from loving, being loved, and acting on that love to perform tasks for others.

THE COUNSELING RELATIONSHIP

It is right that love should be the topic in this first chapter on specific approaches and methods which are useful in helping the person who is struggling with meaninglessness. Love is the essence of all counseling approaches. T'us, all methods need to be loving ones, even those methods which use forms of challenge and confrontation.

A recently divorced client called me not long ago in a state of utter panic. Apparently, he had been out driving and had suddenly seen his ex-wife's car. The sight of it brought a rush of anxiety, grief, and guilt churning in the pit of his stomach, and he turned and headed for home, narrowly avoiding an accident on the way. After listening to him on the phone that Saturday morning, I talked with him about his need to breathe slowly and to sit down awhile before he drove again. Weekends are hard for him now that he is alone. He has a full-time day job and a part-time evening job all week, but on Saturdays and Sundays he has some time to worry. That time was full of terror for him—"I feel like I'm coming unglued," he said. We talked for a few minutes more until his speech rate slowed down and the tension subsided.

In our counseling sessions I had explained the purpose of a support network—people he can call when he needs help. I told him he could call me if he needed to, and he did. He now has a family member, a friend, and me—trusted people he can call if he gets "that wild feeling." None of us provide him with any magic formulas. What he gets from us is a caring voice and unconditional love. I think it is the love that chases away the wild feeling—the feeling that he is out of control, alone in a frightening world, and "coming unglued."

He told me he was going to paint some rooms in his house "just because it needed to be done," but his real purpose was to occupy his weekend time. I then reminded him that his children were coming to visit him in a few weeks. He began to connect the two events and to accept that the task of painting had meaning because it was an act of love to make his children's visit more comfortable. He closed the conversation by saying he would sit awhile and go through his mail, then he would go buy the paint.

Definition of Love

Rollo May defines love as "a delight in the presence of the other person and an affirming of his value development as much as one's own."[1] M. Scott Peck brings in the spiritual dimension to his definition, "The will to extend one's self for the purpose of nurturing one's own or another's spiritual growth."[2] It seems to me the meaning attached to love by biblical writers is not far from Peck's definition. In his letter to the church at Corinth, Paul described love as patient and kind, not jealous, boastful, arrogant, or rude. Love, he said, does not insist on its own way, but seeks justice. It bears all things, believes all things, hopes all things, and endures all things.

Still, it is precisely in trying to nurture another's spiritual growth that we can deceive ourselves. I think of a couple who came for marriage counseling. Like most of the couples I counsel, they came from widely differing backgrounds. She was from a warm, emotionally close, spiritual family. He grew up in a cold, aloof, very "religious" family. His family was at church "every time the doors were open," and his parents demanded that all the children attend the services and sit together as a family. The big emphasis at home was on work and discipline. They talked about love, but "there wasn't any there." Most of the time, he said, his parents talked about God's judgment, and "they whipped me a lot." He lived for one thing—to get out of that family. He left when he graduated from high school. Those parents, I'm sure, simply wanted to nurture their son's spiritual growth. Yet, as Morton Kelsey says, "Love taught by harshness engenders harshness, not love."[3]

Now the husband and wife, both thirty, have vastly different goals for their marriage. She wants to be close; closeness to him is stifling. She wants him to take some responsibility at home; he wants to be free to make the choices he never had the chance to make while growing up. His wife, their children, and he, too, are all paying for his old "emotional debt" caused by the iron hand which his parents equated with God's judgment and a lack of the loving acceptance necessary to develop meaning in his life.

Love is defined, of course, not by so many words but by the things we do and say to each other every day—and by the things we don't say and do. And this is true in the counseling relationship as well as in a family. Love is the path for healing. If the counselor, by the power of the Holy Spirit, can show loving acceptance to the client, the counselor will become a conduit for the healing love of God. There is a great deal more that happens in a counseling session, but nothing happens that is *more important.*

One of the implications here is that if we find ourselves disliking a client, we would do well to refer him or her to another counselor. I don't always like clients. And if that feeling remains unchanged after prayer, I refer the client to someone else. There are some people who say they can love someone without liking him. I think that's true, but the problem is the other person usually feels the dislike rather than the love.

THE SIGNIFICANCE OF LOVE IN THE COUNSELING RELATIONSHIP

Henri Nouwen has placed our love for others in a theological perspective. He has said that it is imperative to keep reminding ourselves that the first and greatest commandment is that we love God with our entire selves.[4] He also questions whether we really believe this. Rather, we seem to love others with our whole selves and have to work hard at not forgetting God. But Jesus clearly prioritizes the two commandments. As Nouwen reminds us, "He asks for a single-minded commitment to God and God alone."[5] Our love for others springs from this wholehearted love for God. If we are to love our clients in the unconditional way that brings healing to them, we need to first love God above all others.

Thirty-five years ago, my wife and I were married in Baltimore. It was a small informal wedding which had been arranged by some of my army buddies. For a wedding present, the couple who stood with us gave us Henry Drummond's little book *The Greatest Thing in the World.*[6] This classic mini-commentary on 1 Corinthians 13 contains the explanation for the meaning of love. "You will find as you look back on your life," Drummond says, "that the moments that stand out, the moments when you have really lived, are the moments when you have done things in a spirit of love."[7] In the booklet, Drummond also mentions the importance of doing unnoticed kindnesses. He tells of looking back over his own life and seeing four or five small acts of love that he did

" . . . standing out above all the life that has gone—Everything else in all our lives is transitory."[8] *This* is the meaning of love, and it is the only thing that lasts.

The interventions in the chapters that follow are useful and can make a difference in the lives of your clients. However, these interventions will have lasting meaning for your clients and for you only as they are done in the spirit of love—the spirit of Christ.

CHAPTER FIVE

COUNSELING AS RELEASING

TAKE A FEW MOMENTS and try to put together a one-sentence definition of counseling that accurately describes what you do. My own definitions have changed over the years, but each one has helped me to center my aim and simplify my effort in the counseling process.

For the last several years, I have defined what I attempt to do as follows: "Counseling is the process whereby clients are released to do what they need to do." Most people who come for counseling are immobilized by suffering, evil, meaninglessness, or other overwhelming causes. They are functioning with only a fraction of the power that is available to them. They need to be released. Jesus said, "So if the Son sets you free, you will be free indeed" (John 8:36 NIV). When Jesus at the beginning of his ministry identified with Isaiah's messianic prophecy, two of the key phrases he quoted were "to proclaim freedom" and "to release the oppressed" (Luke 4:18 NIV).

If releasing people was such an important goal of the ministry of Jesus, should it be any less important in our own? One reason that freedom is so crucial is that it makes responsibility possible. Only free people are able to become responsible. And it is in this responding to life—making choices and taking action—that we discover meaning. With this goal of releasing people in mind, we will now look at the things we should and should not be doing in the counseling process. First, let's explore the interventions that are better left undone.

COUNSELING INTERVENTIONS THAT DO NOT RELEASE

Deception. Deception by the counselor violates the basic principle of honesty in communication. For example, the counselor who uses paradoxical intention must do so with care. I explain the process carefully (see chapter 10) to the client. I also explain that I will ask them to do some things that are opposite to their intentions in counseling and that will require them to face their deepest fears. The rationale for my "strange" request is that the feared reaction is deeply habituated and needs to be jolted out of its hold on the client. By using this approach I have felt comfortable with paradoxical intention. In counseling in general I try to make explicit and implicit that the basis for our work is direct, straightforward communication. If I did not give the rationale for a paradoxical request, I would be "tricking" the client. This could violate the integrity of the relationship.

Manipulation. Another intervention that binds instead of frees is manipulation of the client. An example of client manipulation would be to assign a "homework" task that violates the client's moral standards. Some counselors have suggested to their sexually inhibited clients that they go out and begin a sexual relationship with someone. That request, of course, is manipulative as well as unethical.

The counselor-client relationship is either closed or open. In a closed relationship the counselor does things *for* the client, and sometimes *to* the client. In an open relationship the counselor works from an attitude of great respect for the human dignity of the client and, therefore, sees counseling as working *with* the client. This "withness" is an indispensable aspect of existential counseling. As Rollo May has noted, "In contrast to the psychologies that conclude with theories about conditioning, mechanisms of behavior, and instinctual drives, I maintain that we must go below these theories and discover the person, *the being to whom these things happen.*"[1]

Non-involvement. A depressed client comes to a counselor seeking some release from pain. The counselor may remain detached from this suffering client because of an inability to tolerate the pain of someone close. The client senses the counselor's non-involvement, and now feels rejection in addition to suffering.

The counselor cannot sit on the bleachers in the stadium of life and direct clients in a robot-like fashion. The releasing process described in this book requires that we get into the arena with them and their lion. When we do this, we will begin to understand why clients are frightened and are resisting change. We have to join clients in order to get close enough to release them. Once we have connected with clients through an honest, non-manipulative approach, we can work in several ways to release them.

COUNSELING INTERVENTIONS THAT RELEASE

Released to See Reality Clearly. Frankl has said that the effective counselor is not one who paints a picture so the client sees what to do, but rather is like an opthalmologist who helps the client see things as they are.[2] A definition of mental health is that we live, at whatever cost, in the real world. Releasing questions that can correct a client's vision of himself or herself may include, "If you had what you wanted in life, what would you have?" and "Suppose you take the risk and fail, what is the worst thing that could happen to you?"

A man called to talk about the suffering he and his wife were feeling because their eighteen-year-old daughter was dating a boy whom they intensely disliked. They then came to a counseling session bringing the daughter, her older sister, and her younger brother. The daughter worked in another town and did not live at home. Even so, the pain which her relationship caused her parents was so intense that it was tearing the family apart. She did not want to go home on weekends or vacations because of the anger that was either expressed or atmospheric. Her parents no longer looked forward to her visits with joyful anticipation, but rather with a sadness and dread. In addition, the other siblings began isolating themselves to seek safety from the crossfire. And so the family ties were being stretched and weakened.

I worked first to discover individual and family strengths, and a strong relational theme emerged early in the first session. Different family members were wistfully saying things like, "We used to be a close family," and "We really used to care about each other." Once this theme was made explicit, I began to challenge them on the priority of their values. "Is your love for each other more important than your present disagreement, or do you love and care about and talk kindly to each other only when you are in agreement?" I asked. Their answer to this question was the first step toward seeing the reality of the situation. The parents then began to talk about their fears for their daughter. They were already grieving for the suffering they were sure their daughter would endure if she married her boyfriend. Then the father said to her, "I know I've been driving you into his arms because I wouldn't talk with you."

During the remainder of that session and in the two sessions that followed, we worked to increase the level of listening in the family and to deal with the fear and anger. We also attended to the needs of the two other siblings. After three sessions, I saw no need for further counseling. The family members were able to express their pain to each other and the daughter was coming home more frequently, although she was still dating the boy. The father called me six months later to express appreciation for the counseling. He said that the family situation was continuing to improve, and he expressed his relief that their daughter had broken up with her boyfriend soon after the counseling was ended, even though ending the relationship was very painful for her. She said that *she* decided that they were not suited for each other.

My goal in the counseling was to release the family to see reality clearly. Fear and anger had constricted each member's peripheral vision. Their family life had lost meaning for them because they had lost sight of their priorities. They needed to see and reaffirm the high value which they placed as a family on loving and caring for each other.

Released to Be Oneself. My own introduction to the concept of meaning as a major dimension of life came from reading Paul Tournier's book *The Meaning of Persons*[3] about thirty years ago. I remember puzzling over his concept of "personage," the mask that many of us wear. "We are the slaves of the personage which we have invented for ourselves or which has been imposed on us by others," Tournier said.[4] Much earlier, Blaise Pascal had stated that "we are full of things which take us out of ourselves."[5] Thus, an important part of being released is to take off the masks and, usually with considerable fear, just be ourselves.

Earlier I mentioned that I had been doing Self-Directed Learning Projects for many years. One of the most exciting was one I called Learning from Children. I have collected over a thousand stories from adults concerning what they have learned from children. The most significant aspect of the project for me was finding that the outstanding quality of children is their *vulnerability.* Little children have not learned to be anything other than what they are. They are still free. Most of us are not, so we need to be released from the masks which society has led us to believe we need. This needs to be done lovingly and gently. You can't get a turtle to stick its neck out by banging on the shell!

What can the counselor do to release clients in this area? People are more likely to be themselves if they feel safe, and if, in that secure place, they are challenged. The counselor provides such a place by respecting the dignity of the client. In turn, this respect generates trust. But that is not enough. The counselor needs to confront gently those parts of the person that are dissonant and do not belong. When a good friend said to me twenty years ago, "Paul, you always have to have the last word," I realized he was also saying, "and that's not you." Because of this gentle, direct confrontation from a friend with

44

whom I felt safe, I began to change this competitive way of ending a conversation. I have become more me, more whole, by sloughing off this abrasive behavior.

Released to Love and Be Loved. Once we see reality clearly and we find more and more release to become the persons God created and redeemed us to be, we are closer to being released to love and be loved. And this is perhaps the greatest freedom for which we can be instrumental in helping our clients achieve. This release is made possible by healing and by spiritual growth. Spiritual growth is not as "natural" an outcome of counseling as is healing. Healing, after all, is what counseling is all about. Clients come because they are suffering and they need healing.

Once there has been some healing, it is easy to send clients on their way without attending to spiritual growth. However, we owe it to our clients to assist with the development of their spiritual maturity. If a client has not brought up the subject, I usually do so by asking, "What are your spiritual resources for dealing with predicaments like this?" or "How is your spiritual life going?" Often clients will respond with statements regarding whether or not they are going to church. I then tell them that I am also interested in the depth of their *personal relationship* with God. This process takes some time, but it often reveals entire areas of needed growth, such as forgiveness, prayer, Bible reading and study, Christian fellowship, and renewal. When the client has targeted and made some progress in one or two such needy areas, both the counselor and the client can end counseling with greater confidence about the future.

CHAPTER SIX

THE EXISTENTIAL APPROACH TO COUNSELING

WHAT IS YOUR counseling style? Probably it is based squarely on your lifestyle. One way to learn more about your "style" is to complete the Responding-Style Checklist, shown in figure 1. The results of the checklist will help you to discover how you are likely to respond to your friends and others close to you.

Simply go down each column, checking those items that are typically true of you. Then tally the number of check marks in each column. Add the checks in all five columns, divide by five, and you will thus obtain an "average." If the checks in any column total two or three above the average, this indicates a strength. The checklist is not a scientific instrument, but it may give you some clues. If you are strong in the *sensing* area,

Responding-Style Checklist[1]

I. SENSES

— 1. You usually take time to eat slowly and to taste your food.
— 2. You like to have people touch you.
— 3. You usually concentrate carefully on what others tell you.
— 4. You listen to music for all the nuances, not just the melody.
— 5. You find it easy to touch people, especially those who are psychologically close to you.
— 6. You enjoy the fragrance of food.
— 7. You literally take time to smell the flowers.
— 8. You listen to others' voice inflections and variations to catch deeper meanings.
— 9. You "listen with your eyes," i.e., you observe facial movements and gestures of others to catch deeper meanings.
— 10. You are able effectively to "tune out" background sounds and listen accurately to the person who is talking.

II. EMOTIONS

— 1. Someone has told you in the last six months that he/she appreciates your warmth.
— 2. You usually are able to express angry feelings.
— 3. It is natural and easy for you to maintain eye contact with a person to whom you are talking.
— 4. You enjoy receiving compliments and react graciously.
— 5. You've been angry at someone in the last few weeks.
— 6. You've told someone within the last week that you appreciate, like, or love him/her.
— 7. Others see you as a friendly person, easy to get to know.
— 8. You smile as much or more than most people.
— 9. You rarely use sarcasm.
— 10. You often share your deep feelings with others.

III. THOUGHTS

— 1. You usually consider consequences before acting.
— 2. You usually plan purchases well in advance and resist buying on impulse.
— 3. You are prompt for appointments.
— 4. You can visualize the results of your actions easily.
— 5. You usually plan ahead and avoid predicaments.
— 6. When you have a task to do, you typically do it rather than avoid it.
— 7. You would classify yourself as dependable rather than undependable.
— 8. It seems to be easier for you than for most to stay within a budget.
— 9. At a restaurant you rarely order more than you can eat.
— 10. You find it easy to think through your day tomorrow.

IV. CHOICES

— 1. You make important decisions easily and decisively, rather than spend a lot of time worrying about them.
— 2. You prefer to make your own decisions.
— 3. You usually have a clear sense of what is right and wrong.
— 4. Life has a great deal of meaning for you.
— 5. You have clear-cut personal goals.
— 6. You can usually find the courage to make the decisions you need to.
— 7. Right now you're finding it fairly easy to decide which of these areas you're strong in.
— 8. You could quickly and easily list three or four values in life that are very important to you.
— 9. Courage ranks high in your value system.
— 10. You feel confident of your decision-making ability.

V. ACTIONS

— 1. You generally live in the present by forgetting the past and not worrying about the future.
— 2. You are involved in life and rarely spend time "feeling miserable."
— 3. You typically find it easy to sleep at night.
— 4. Overall, you feel confident about your future.
— 5. You see yourself as a competent person.
— 6. You usually feel healthy and full of energy.
— 7. It is easy to concentrate on what you are reading.
— 8. You usually finish what you start.
— 9. You enjoy beginning the day.
— 10. You view difficult circumstances as challenges rather than insurmountable obstacles.

Figure 1

you will probably be effective in connecting rapidly with the person experiencing emotional trauma. If you are strong in the *emotions* channel, you will be especially useful in helping your friend work through feelings. If you are strong in the *thinking* channel, you can help your friend analyze the situation and visualize the consequences. If *choosing* is your forte, you can serve as a model in this process. And if *action* is your strong point, you will emphasize by your life how to spend energy on getting things done rather than brooding about them.[2]

Let us suppose that your results from this checklist confirm what you already thought was your strong responding-style channel. To add more meaning to this discovery, take a look at figure 2, Some Therapeutic Methods Using Different Response Channels. Compare your strong channel to the approaches shown in figure 2. Are you more attracted to those methods that involve your strong channel?

Some Therapeutic Methods Using Different Responding Channels				
I. SENSES	II. EMOTIONS	III. THOUGHTS	IV. CHOICES	V. ACTIONS
Breathing Therapies	Client-Centered Therapy (Carl Rogers)	Psychoanalysis (Sigmund Freud)	Existential Therapies (Rollo May, Irvin Yalom, Adrian van Kaam)	Behavior Therapy (Joseph Wolpe)
Massage	Gestalt Therapy (Fritz Perls)	Rational-Emotive Therapy (Albert Ellis)		
Relaxation Therapies (Herbert Benson)			Logotherapy (Viktor Frankl)	Reinforcement Theory and Psychoanalytic Therapy (John Dollard and Neal Miller)
Therapeutic Touch (Dolores Krieger)		Transactional Analysis (Eric Berne)	Reality Therapy (William Glasser)	

Figure 2

The names accompanying most of the methods are the founders of that approach, except for those shown with relaxation and existential therapies. With those therapies the names are those of one or more of many therapists utilizing that approach. For instance, Herbert Benson is an M.D. and therefore very interested in the body and the physical senses.[3] Carl

Rogers's life and interpersonal style was characterized by his attention to emotions and his sensitivity. I once heard him speak and was impressed by his tenderness. It is therefore not surprising to me that out of this strength he built the entire "school" of client-centered counseling in which the main focus is on feelings and emotions.

The divisions shown in figure 2 are not meant to be rigid. Most practitioners have used several, if not all, of the channels. However, they typically use their strong channel to *connect* with their clients. For example, Fritz Perls used anger in his counseling. His counseling verbatims make this clear.[4] He was able to connect with people and to bring about change by his use of anger.

Psychoanalysis relies heavily on the thinking channel. Sigmund Freud was known for his analytical mind, not his relational approach to life. He worked hard to elicit insight. Albert Ellis also relies on the cognitive approach. A client, for instance, says that an expected future event will be "dreadful." Ellis may respond, "No, it would only be inconvenient." In truth, there aren't that many dreadful things!

Existential therapist Rollo May was in a life and death struggle with tuberculosis in a sanatorium for eighteen months. He made the choice to live. Viktor Frankl also came to value the power of choice in a life-threatening situation. Thus, it is natural that they emphasize choice to their clients. In a larger sense, all the approaches in the Choices column fall under the existential heading.

Psychiatrist Joseph Wolpe grew disenchanted with psychoanalysis. He then studied Pavlov. Wolpe did a great many animal experiments and deepened his interest in the stimulus-response approach to behavior change.

Each of the above practitioners had personal as well as professional reasons for adopting his approach to behavior change. So do we. As we study our lifestyles, we will probably discover that our counseling style is built squarely on them. Most Christian counselors would probably best fit under the existential "choice" heading. They fit there, not because they agree with all the beliefs of the other existential counselors, but because they emphasize the client's need to respond to

God, that is, to choose. The title of Frank Minirth and Paul Meier's book, *Happiness Is a Choice*, is a clear illustration of this approach.[5]

THE CHOICE CHANNEL—THE EXISTENTIAL APPROACH

Irvin Yalom's book, *Existential Psychotherapy*, is a thorough, carefully documented treatment of the subject.[6] His lengthy coverage of various topics provides a road map to the major points of existential counseling. "This book deals with four ultimate concerns: death, freedom, isolation, and meaninglessness," he says.[7] Yalom also declares the first three of these concerns must be dealt with directly.[8] However, with meaninglessness "the effective therapist must help patients to look *away* from the question . . . ."[9] The counselor's tool is engagement, "a leap into commitment and action."[10] We discover meaning when we respond to life. According to Yalom, the counselor helps the client become engaged with life by forming a close counselor-client relationship.[11]

Yalom asked an important question: "Where in professional training curriculums does the therapist learn about . . . meaninglessness, or about psychotherapeutic strategies available to assist patients in a crisis of meaning?"[12] Since many counselor training programs are silent in this crucial area, I hope this book will help fill the gap for both beginning and experienced counselors.

Of the many books which focus on choice, certainly the Bible is the most important. It is an existential book. The call to choose is issued throughout the Old Testament, with this command standing out: "Choose for yourselves this day whom you will serve . . . " (Josh. 24:15 NIV). And this focus on choice continues throughout the New Testament, right on to the last chapter of the book of Revelation, "Come, whoever is thirsty; accept the water of life as a gift, whoever wants it" (Rev. 22:17 TEV). We are free to choose to accept or not to accept.

This book on counseling those who search for meaning in life emphasizes the existential approach to counseling. But what if this is not your strong channel? Look back for a moment to the Responding-Style Checklist on page 47 to see how you did. If the *choice* channel is not one of your strengths, using this approach may not be natural to you at first. But this need not be an insurmountable barrier. My own strong channel as estimated by this checklist is *emotions*. So working with the existential approach has been something I've had to work at over the years. I think I've made considerable progress, and I believe you can, too.

Most effective counseling approaches require that we begin by understanding clients' feelings and letting them know that we understand. But this approach, while an excellent place to start, is not a good place to end. In fact, if the counseling ends there, it may actually be counter-productive because clients are left even more deeply immersed in their problems. Fabry notes that the existential counselor, especially the logotherapist, challenges clients "to make choices, accept responsibilities and commitments, and take steps—be they ever so small—in a new direction, away from the problem."[13]

We need to be flexible as we work with different clients, and even with the same client in different treatment stages. However, this does not imply that the existential counselor is eclectic. The different techniques arise out of the same method. The clear aim is to call the client to a *decision to respond to life*. This response must be achieved by the discovery process so the client can be fully committed to it.

CHAPTER SEVEN

THE CONTRIBUTIONS OF
VIKTOR FRANKL

VIKTOR FRANKL WAS BORN in 1905 in Vienna. When he was nineteen he published his first article, at the invitation of Sigmund Freud, in the *International Journal of Psychoanalysis*. He received an M.D. degree from the University of Vienna when he was twenty-five. In the early 1930s he founded youth counseling centers in Austria. Many of the youth who came to these centers were disillusioned because they were unable to find jobs during the widespread economic depression of those years. Joseph Fabry, the Director of the Institute of Logotherapy at Berkeley, California, and a friend of Frankl's, noted that Frankl began formulating his idea that all of life has meaning as he worked with these

52

youth.[1] Frankl found that the despair of these youth could be relieved by giving them tasks to accomplish, even though the jobs were nonpaying. He began to see that despair was suffering in which the sufferer could not find meaning. "But meaning can be found in a much wider range than the sufferer realizes, and it is the task of the therapist to widen the patient's horizon, to expose the patient to the full range of meaning possibilities," he wrote.[2]

During World War II, Frankl spent three years in German concentration camps. Frankl has told the "pain-full," "meaning-full" story of these years in his book *Man's Search for Meaning*. While in the death camps, Frankl refined his notion of the value of attitudinal change. "We had to learn ourselves and, furthermore, we had to teach the despairing men, that *it did not really matter what we expected from life, but rather what life expected from us.*"[3] The important thing, Frankl said, is that our answer has to be given not in words, but in responsible action.

What did life expect of Frankl in the camps? He helped in the organization and delivery of an underground health (including mental health) delivery system. For example, he helped prevent two suicide attempts by asking the men what life asked of them. One of these men then chose to live for his child, and the other chose to live to complete a task, a series of scientific books. Frankl noted, therefore, that both human love and creative work can give meaning to life.[4]

Frankl has documented his journey away from psychoanalysis in his book *The Doctor and the Soul*.[5] His life and writings have shown that both reductionism and nihilism are wrong and dangerous. Reductionism is the view that humans are motivated only by biological, instinctual drives, defense mechanisms, or conditioning (stimulus-response) processes. Freud reduced human motivation to a sense of "drivenness" with his postulation of the pleasure principle. B. F. Skinner did the same thing with his view of the power of operant conditioning. Frankl wrote regarding reductionism: "Doesn't it sound somewhat like, Seek ye first the kingdom of Freud and Skinner, and all these things will be added unto you?"[6]

Nihilism is the view that life is useless and meaningless and, therefore, that traditional beliefs and values are without foundation. Frankl reserves his strongest condemnation for this philosophy of life. He said that the gas chambers in which millions of Jews were killed "were ultimately prepared not in some Ministry or other in Berlin, but rather at the desks and in the lecture halls of nihilistic scientists and philosophers."[7]

Nihilists say they believe that we live in a world in which nothing matters. If nothing matters, then life is not worth living. Yalom has pointed out a logical inconsistency in the nihilist position: "For one thing, if nothing matters, it should not matter that nothing matters."[8] In actuality, nihilistic philosophers have worked very hard to write books and in other ways promulgate their views. It does seem to have mattered to them that nothing matters.

Frankl's experiences confirmed his belief that, in contrast to reductionism and nihilism, our chief motivation is the quest to find a meaning in life.[9] This "Third Viennese School of Psychotherapy" is in contrast to the first—Freud's psychoanalysis, with pleasure as the motivator—and the second—Alfred Adler's individual psychology, with social power the motivator.[10]

Frankl has noted that much is made of depth psychology, and has said that now it is time to consider "height psychology," to deal with the spiritual aspects of our clients.[11] We need to emphasize not what is wrong with people, but what is right; not what is missing, but what is left. Instead of trying to unearth his clients' secrets, he helped them discover inner resources and a new direction in life. Three of these resources are crucial in finding meaning.

The first of these is the *spiritual* dimension: "The psychophysical organism is of great importance, but only as the instrument and expression of the real person, manifest through the spiritual dimension," Frankl says.[12] He goes on to say that while the psychophysical organism is useful to us as a tool, the person has value, or worth. And this worth does not depend on usefulness.

A second critical dimension of the person is *freedom*. We are not free to dictate all the conditions of our life. But we are free to take our stand concerning them. Freud stressed determinism, not freedom. Frankl quotes Freud, "Let us attempt to expose a number of the most diverse people uniformly to hunger. With the increase of the imperative urge of hunger all individual differences will blur, and in their stead will appear the uniform expression of the one unstilled urge."[13] Frankl, however, said that when he saw this hypothesis tested in the concentration camps, actually the reverse occurred: "People became more diverse. The beast was unmasked—and so was the saint. The hunger was the same but people were different. In truth, calories do not count."[14]

The last line above echoes the Lord's statement, "Man does not live on bread alone, but on every word that comes from the mouth of God" (Matt. 4:4). After going over a month without food, Jesus was no doubt in an emaciated, starving condition when he faced Satan. Who knows how attractive it would have been to Jesus to turn the stones into bread? But his condition did not predetermine him. He took a stand and made a choice. We are always free to choose, if not our condition, then at least our response or our attitude toward it.

The concept of response is closely tied to a third dimension of life—*responsibility.* Frankl has frequently said that just as we have a Statue of Liberty on the east coast so we should have a Statue of Responsibility on the west coast. Both freedom and responsibility are required for a balanced, whole life. Frankl has noted that psychoanalysis has placed all its emphasis on consciousness, whereas individual (Adlerian) psychology has placed its emphasis on responsibleness. However, he said, "one might state it as a basic theorem that *being human means being conscious and being responsible.*"[15]

Frankl emphasized the importance of becoming responsible rather than merely taking responsibility. This latter concept, significant for effective counseling, is developed more fully in a later chapter. Frankl's major contribution, of course, is his legacy of logotherapy as a system of counseling and how it may be applied. But how about Frankl the person?

All of Frankl's immediate family—parents, siblings, wife, and children—perished during the war, with the exception of one sister. After the war, he remarried and returned to Vienna. In 1946, he became head of the Neurological Policlinic Hospital.

In 1947, he received a professorial appointment at the University of Vienna, and he earned his Ph.D. there in 1949. Throughout his career he has taught there, has written voluminously and usefully, and has lectured in many countries. His presence worldwide has been a reminder that the essence of life is spiritual, and the chief motivation of humankind is to live a life rich with meaning.

Adrian van Kaam has summarized effectively Frankl's response to suffering. He observed that Frankl was a victim of a cruel regime. "It seems poetic justice that in the camps of deformation and degradation, he tested a conception of human life that made the will to meaning a basic condition for its free and full unfolding."[16]

How do Frankl's views fit with Christian beliefs? Donald Tweedie's answer to this question may be found in his book *Logotherapy and the Christian Faith.* Tweedie concludes that the Christian counselor will need to go beyond the teachings of logotherapy "in order to satisfy the responsibility entailed in a biblical vocation. He will be greatly encouraged by Frankl's work."[17]

Frankl has been careful to point out that his is not a religious system. He has used the analogy of a train ride to describe the search for meaning. Logotherapy, he says, does not provide ultimate answers—final stations. Rather, "it leads patients, the religious as well as the non-religious, to a point where they can find their own transfers to stations beyond, to their own ultimate station."[18]

Irvin Yalom, in his book *Existential Psychotherapy,* has disagreed with Frankl on the religious issue: "Furthermore, though he claims to present a secular approach to meaning . . . it is clear that Frankl's approach to meaning is fundamentally religious."[19] Yalom also distinguishes between "cosmic meaning" and "terrestrial meaning."[20] Cosmic meaning "implies some design existing outside of and superior to the person and invariably refers to some magical or spiritual ordering of the universe."[21] Terrestrial meaning may "have foundations that are entirely secular—that is, one may have a personal sense of meaning without a cosmic meaning system."[22]

I think Yalom's differentiation is correct because I have

known many people who have a personal sense of meaning that is not related to cosmic meaning. But in times of crisis, of deep reflection, and when facing death, one yearns for cosmic or ultimate meaning. The secular meaning is not enough. I agree also with Yalom that Frankl's view is basically religious because it has to do with the discovery of ultimate meaning, and is, therefore, spiritual. Because the basis of Frankl's views has the same common ground as our Judeo-Christian roots—we are spiritual beings—and because meaning is seen as our chief motivation, many Christian counselors have found his methods useful additions to their repertoire.

Robert Leslie, the author of *Jesus as Counselor*,[23] noted that the philosophy of life and counseling method offered by logotherapy are "more consistent with a basically Christian view of life than any other existing system in the current therapeutic world."[24] Jesus both supported and challenged people. Logotherapy also works in these two ways. And just as the call to choose and act is at the center of the Christian faith, this imperative is also central in Frankl's formulation of logotherapy.

The next few chapters provide systematic ways for applying logotherapy steps and methods. We can utilize Frankl's approach, and go beyond it as Christian counselors. We go beyond it when we counsel out of our perspective of the Christian faith. The following questions may help sharpen that perspective: What does life expect of me at this point in my journey? How does my relationship with Christ affect the way I counsel? How could I help a client relieve his or her despair by discovering a meaningful task to do? Am I emphasizing *both* freedom and responsibility in my counseling?

CHAPTER EIGHT

THE LOGOTHERAPY APPROACH

LOGOTHERAPY SUGGESTS ways of living and ways of counseling. The preceding chapter focused on useful ways of responding to life. This chapter will emphasize the logotherapeutic approach to counseling.

Logotherapy as developed by Frankl and described by him, Joseph Fabry, Elisabeth Lukas, and others, usually suggests four steps (the approach) and three methods (the techniques). These steps and methods vary somewhat with different authors. The methods are technically referred to as Socratic questioning, paradoxical intention, and dereflection. Each of these techniques will be discussed in detail in the following chapters. An important differentiation in the *steps* and *methods* is that the steps are sequential and the methods are not. A counselor may use Socratic questioning, paradoxical intention, and dereflection in any order, or he may use only one or two of these methods with a client.

Understanding the *approach* enables the counselor to form a point of view concerning the purposes and timing of the methods. The steps (as well as the methods) involve attitudinal change. The four-step sequence that provides the map for logotherapeutic counseling includes helping clients distance themselves from their symptoms, finding ways to modify counterproductive attitudes, the resulting reduction or disappearance of symptoms, and guiding the clients in their discovery of greater meaning prior to the termination of counseling.

STEP ONE: HELPING YOUR CLIENT DISTANCE FROM SYMPTOMS

Most people come for counseling because they are suffering. They are anxious, depressed, guilty, grieving, angry, or confused. Their symptoms may include an overwhelming sadness that has lowered the quality of their work, waves of anxiety that keep them hiding out at home, or a wrenching bitterness that results in sarcasm and other attacks of verbal violence on those they love. How can we as Christian counselors help clients put distance between themselves and their symptoms?

One of the most useful books I've read on counseling is *Meaning in Suffering,* by Elisabeth Lukas.[1] In it she discusses the importance of this step. Clients, she says, are the victims of an illness if they have identified with it. This is true whether they use the fight or the flight response in dealing with it. Therefore, logotherapy's first step requires the counselor "to arouse and strengthen in patients their capacity for self-distance because this is the basis of a healthy resistance in a crisis; self-distancing means, among other things, to smile at oneself."[2]

Most major counseling approaches require the counselor to focus on the clients' problems and to do this at deeper and deeper levels. Instead of helping clients distance from their symptoms, this approach causes them to identify more and more with their symptoms and perhaps eventually to view themselves as the helpless victims of these symptoms.

William Glasser, the author of *Reality Therapy*, has also pointed out the danger of the counselor spending so much time on the problem itself.[3] Glasser told about an irresponsible nineteen-year-old college student who had discussed his problems for a year with another psychiatrist. Glasser had to make a decision when he took Rob as a client. Rob wanted to dwell on his life history—on his many failures. Glasser refused to listen to this. "I would have necessarily assumed a superior role. A person feels inferior when he tells of his failures and misfortunes unless he is closely involved with the listener."[4] This process degrades and weakens the client. Instead of dwelling on the past, Glasser asked Rob for his plan for a more productive future. A plan, of course, involves choices. So Glasser was taking an existential approach rather than the traditional psychoanalytical approach.

The logotherapist needs to go beyond the problem to ask thought-provoking questions, to speak of hope and meaning, and to use humor when appropriate. The point of view taken here is that we don't always have to know the cause of a fire in order to put it out. One method that is not used, however, is persuasion. Fabry has warned that "the more one tries to persuade patients that, for instance, things are not all that bad or that they 'should' do this or that, the more their resistance is aroused, resulting in a 'yes, but' reaction."[5]

Newton's third law of motion, "For every action there is an equal and opposite reaction," is valid in psychology as well as in physics. When we push clients, they dig in their heels, or they may agree until they are out of our presence. Then they will do whatever they were doing before seeing a counselor.

This chapter provides the rationale for following the steps sequentially. The reason for attending first to distancing from symptoms is that clients often cannot work on the next step—attitudinal change—until they loosen themselves from the grip of the symptom. For example, everyone has experienced physical pain from an injury, illness, or headache and felt somewhat immobilized by that pain. Then something happens, a loved one enters the room, we read an interesting novel, or see an entertaining show, and we focus our attention away from the pain for a bit. It is still there, as we discover later, but for a while we were distanced from it and could function normally. That is the purpose of working on this important first step. We help clients function *as if* the symptoms of depression, for example, were not present. Then they can work on attitudinal change so the symptoms can actually be reduced or eliminated.

STEP TWO: ATTITUDINAL CHANGE

Once clients have achieved some distance from the immobilizing symptoms, the counselor can begin work in the area of attitudes. Attitudinal change is pervasive in logotherapy. It is involved in all the steps and each of the methods. Although it is somewhat artificial to isolate it as one particular step, it is useful to do so for purposes of explanation. Elisabeth Lukas has described the significance of the modification of attitudes. She noted that it is important in the logotherapy approach to counseling, "especially when clients find themselves in situations that are void of meaning yet cannot be changed—'blows of fate,' accidents, incurable disease, the irrevocable ending of a relationship, a career, a life."[6] These events, as tragic and senseless as they are, do not need to control our lives. "It is possible and therapeutic to find a meaningful attitude toward a situation which in itself is meaningless," she continues.[7] This is the important point—that meaning need not be found in the event itself, but may be discovered through a transformed attitude. Dramas are played out on this theme every day, in movies, plays, and real life. One of the most striking was in the life of Frankl himself. For Jews to be placed by Nazis in concentration camps, all to be cruelly treated and most to be killed, was a senseless act. But Viktor Frankl found meaning by refocusing his attitude to the needs of those around him and to the call of future tasks when the war would be over. Like Frankl, we can choose to live our lives according to healthy or unhealthy attitudes.

Healthy attitude: I have freedom.
Unhealthy attitude: I am a victim of "fate."
Healthy attitude: I need to become responsible, to respond

to what life is asking of me, so that I can pay my rent on this earth.

Unhealthy attitude: The chief aim of life is to heighten pleasure and reduce discomfort and suffering.

Healthy attitude: I will live according to my values.

Unhealthy attitude: I will live according to whatever feels good at the moment.

Healthy attitude: Ultimate meaning exists and it can be discovered.

Unhealthy attitude: Life is absurd, and if we are going to find any meaning we will have to invent it ourselves.

Healthy attitude: I need to discover how among all of the five billion people in the world I am unique in terms of my own personality and my mission in life.

Unhealthy attitude: I will spend a great deal of my time comparing myself with others and as a result some of the time I will feel superior and arrogant, and other times I will feel inferior and diminished.

Logotherapists point to self-transcendence as an important way to redirect our lives. Frankl defines self-transcendence as "a cause to serve or a person to love."[8] He is emphatic that "only to the extent that someone is living out this self-transcendence of human existence, is he truly human or does he become his true self."[9] Christian counselors are in a position to provide great hope at this point because the Christian faith provides *both* a cause to serve and a person to love.

STEP THREE: THE ACTUAL REDUCTION OF SYMPTOMS

After the client achieves a radical transformation of attitudes, the symptoms often diminish or disappear as unexplainably as they came.

A twenty-two-year-old woman was referred for counseling because of her anorexia nervosa. Although tall and large-framed, her eating disorder had ravaged her, and her weight had dropped almost 28 percent, from 130 pounds to 94 pounds. Her menstrual period had stopped, but she had refused hospitalization. She still saw herself as overweight. I followed my usual guidelines in eating disorder counseling: Be sure the client is also seeing a physician and a nutritionist, and bring in the family for counseling, as well as do individual counseling if the client desires it.

After hearing her story I told her I was not nearly as interested in the fact that she had deprived herself of physical nourishment as I was in her malnourished condition in the area of meaning. She had stopped reading books and she did not talk about things that had spiritual significance. She was a Christian, and I'm sure she knew somewhere deep inside that she could not live by bread alone, whether much or little. I shared some books with her, including Bruce Larson's *There's a Lot More to Health Than Not Being Sick.*[10] She began reading from the Gospel of John. And she loaned me one or two of her books. All of these materials were grist for the mill of conversation.

We usually talked about food when she came with her family because her weight loss was, of course, their primary concern. She worked hard and her family worked hard to open, clean, and suture some old wounds. This enabled her to feel good about leaving home, rather than just "getting out of that place." She even gained some weight before going to an out-of-state college. We corresponded during the academic year, and we talked a few times during her vacations. When she dropped by to see me briefly the next summer, she was at her old weight of 130 pounds. When I asked how she saw her body now, she said, "I still see myself as fat, but it doesn't make any difference anymore." She wrote intermittently after that, and sent a picture several years later of herself, her husband, and their new baby. Her symptoms were reduced, I believe, because she changed her attitude and saw that she needed to attend to her spiritual nourishment. By doing this she was able to choose life again and to care for all her needs, including those of her body. One of the most thorough and useful books for counselors on the subject of eating disorders is *Counseling Those with Eating Disorders,* by Raymond E. Vath.[11]

STEP FOUR: AN ORIENTATION TO MEANING BEFORE TERMINATING COUNSELING

The logical thing to do when the client's symptoms no longer interfere with functioning is for the counselor or client to terminate counseling. This is a mistake. Elisabeth Lukas has warned that "the entire therapy is jeopardized if the patient is discharged to a life lacking meaningful content."[12] She suggests that this final phase "requires that counselor and client go on a common search to discover a variety of ways to find meanings, to reconstruct existence, to appraise opportunities, and see the direction life is to take."[13]

The first three steps, described above—distancing from symptoms, modifying attitudes, and the actual reduction of symptoms—are chiefly useful in remedying the predicament or crisis. Now that's not bad. But it stops short of what is needed. Symptoms serve a purpose. They are often a dysfunctional way to keep us from "falling apart." An alcoholic who has stopped drinking still has to find a way to face each day. Terminating counseling before attending to meaning orientation is somewhat analogous to the man Jesus talked about who had been cleansed of an evil spirit, but because he remained "unoccupied," the evil spirit returns with "seven other spirits more wicked than itself, and they go in and live there. And the final condition of that man is worse than the first" (Matt. 12:45 NIV).

So before we terminate the counseling, we should be sure the client is not just empty of symptoms but is also filled with a sense of mission and meaning in life, or at least is aware of an emerging, meanful direction in life. Often this comes through discussions of values, biblical passages, challenges, relationships, and spiritual concerns. The pastor or Christian counselor thus acts through the power of the Holy Spirit to help empty the client of symptoms and then fill the client with meaning. It is important to not send people away empty. Specific guidelines for this fourth step are given in chapter 32.

There are frequent references throughout the rest of this book to the above four steps. As one of the three primary logotherapy methods or another technique is applied to a given situation, there will often be a reference noting the particular logotherapy step that is being taken. These later references will help build a sense of both the importance and the sequential nature of the steps.[14]

CHAPTER NINE

SOCRATIC QUESTIONING

THE GREAT TEACHERS have always been question-askers. Effective counselors also have this skill, especially those who are concerned with meaning. In his book on logotherapy, Joseph Fabry gives a concise rationale for this approach. "Logotherapy has demonstrated repeatedly that the effect of answers about life's meaning are incomparably deeper if they come from the patient, not from the therapist."[1]

In order for answers to come from the client, the counselor needs to occasionally ask questions. I use "occasion" here in its primary dictionary definition, "a favorable opportunity or circumstance." If questions are asked too often, they become counter-productive because they wear people out, are felt as interrogative, and place the questioner firmly in control (and the questioned out of control). The counselor needs to be alert for "a favorable opportunity."

Although all counseling theorists and practitioners use some questions, Frankl has most effectively built upon an old method, the Socratic dialogue. He has refined this technique to provide counselors some guidelines for noting the opportune moment to ask questions, and for effectively phrasing those questions. Socratic questions were, of course, named for Socrates, but were asked long before the fifth century, B.C. Socratic questions are questions that *draw out* thoughtful, substantive, meaningful answers. The questioner is characterized by honesty, directness, and a sense of what is significant in life. Such questions were, much later, given Socrates's name because he was world class in their use.

Some examples of actual logotherapeutic questions can be found in the case studies reported by Frankl and others. Dr. Elisabeth Lukas is a psychologist and is Director of the Southern German Institute of Logotherapy. She shares many Socratic questions in her excellent book, *Meaningful Living*.[2] She did her doctoral work under Viktor Frankl and is now one of the leaders of the logotherapy movement. She tells of counseling a woman who had "everything." Yet the woman spent much of her day in bed and was pitied by those who loved her. Dr. Lukas suspected she did not want to be cured, that she "needed" to be sick. So she asked her the following thought-provoking, image-producing question:

"You stand among the flowers and water the weeds," I once told the patient, and she laughed. "That's exactly what I do," she said.
"Why?" I kept asking. "Why?"
"That's why I come to you," she said. "You water the flowers, I water the weeds."[3]

This is a powerful example of a Socratic question. A question such as this, because of the image it creates, will stimulate the clients' thinking long after the session is over. Such a question is valuable in achieving the first step in logotherapy—distancing from the symptoms because of its "light touch" and humor.

One psychologist claims the central question in crisis therapy is "What do *you* want to do with your life?"[4] He goes on to say that "It is a question that must be asked in as many ways as the therapist can devise until the patient becomes oriented to its validity."[5] The ultimate aim of these questions by Lukas and LeShan, and indeed all Socratic questioners, is to help the client become responsible, i.e., able to respond to life.

For the last several years I have been developing a list of conversational topics designed to help clients talk about subjects of concern to them. The list is shown in figure 3.[6] They are phrased as the beginning of sentences. I have often given clients the list and asked them to choose a "front-burner" topic. At other times just thinking of some of the items on the list has helped me phrase questions. It is easy to go from the topics to questions. Number 2 becomes "What is a personal quality or strength you cherish about yourself?" Number 12 could be "Would you please describe a relationship that means a lot to you?" And Number 27, "What is the most creative thing you do?"

These questions work well to get a meaningful conversation going. Once you and the client are deeply involved in a conversation about meaning, you will need to "think on your feet" to come up with relevant questions for the place where the client is at any given time. The questions should bring the client not just to insight, but to a choice. Fabry illustrates the difference between the two aims of insight and choice. He was struggling with past tragedies and the need for healing. Healing didn't come through an insight question, "Why did it happen to me?" Rather, healing started to occur with a question that required a choice, "Granted that there are chance and injustice in the world, what can I—and sometimes only I—do in the situation in which I find myself?"[7] Such a question can be useful in several of the logotherapy steps, but particularly in step two—the modification of attitudes.

Topics That Evoke Meaningful Conversations

Many of the coversation topics below are spiritual without being religious. They are topics that matter. Most are clear enough, except perhaps numbers 5 and 21. Sid Simon says that a cookie person is someone, usually in our early lives, who loved us unconditionally and invested time and attention in us. A mentor is someone we select as a one-to-one teacher to guide us in some specific area, for example, developing our tennis skills or learning Spanish.

1. A goal that's important to me is . . . .
2. A personal quality or strength I cherish about myself is . . . .
3. A predicament I'm facing is . . . .
4. A memory that stands out is . . . .
5. A cookie person in my early life was . . . .
6. A joy in my life right now is . . . .
7. A dream (quest) I would like to have come true someday is . . . .
8. A regret I need to deal with is . . . .
9. A challenge before me is . . . .
10. A fear I would like to be free of is . . . .
11. My self worth is . . . .
12. A relationship that means a lot to me is . . . .
13. A concern I have is . . . .
14. I would like to celebrate . . . .
15. One of my most important beliefs is . . . .

16. A thing (object) that has a lot of meaning is . . . .
17. An accomplishment that I feel good about is . . . .
18. A person I need to say "I love you" to is . . . .
19. My listening ability is . . . .
20. I find courage by . . . .
21. A mentor of mine is (or was) . . . .
22. A part of me that needs healing is . . . .
23. Something I need to change, but that I'm resisting changing is . . . .
24. I'm surprised that . . . .
25. A helping skill that I have is . . . .
26. My spiritual growth is . . . .
27. The most creative thing I do is . . . .
28. I feel most renewed when . . . .
29. Someone who would name me as his or her mentor is . . . .
30. When I look to the future, I . . . .

Figure 3

SOCRATIC DIALOGUE

The counselor's Socratic questions and the client's responses to these questions make up a Socratic dialogue. Dr. James Yoder, a psychologist in Kansas City, has noted that "Socratic dialogue aims at heightening self-awareness, deepening the look within. It helps clients verify their most defining attribute, 'freedom.'"[8] This is the genius of Socratic dialogue. When clients discover their freedom, they can begin to be responsible. It is when people feel predetermined that they are irresponsible—not able to respond.

Yoder makes the point that Socratic dialogue should be specific. He notes some Socratic questions from actual counseling sessions: "What did you feel?" rather than "How did you feel?" "What does the present situation demand?"[9] "*Something keeps you from behaving this way. What is it?*" "*What did you discover from that experience?*" "*What are you learning about yourself as you experience this very human struggle?*"[10] By such questions, Yoder says, "the counselor urges the client to look beneath the surface, not to be content with generalities and quick explanations about his behavior."[11] Therefore, it may be seen that Socratic dialogue produces *depth* in the conversation.

Socratic questions need to be asked that stretch the thinking of the client. This requires very careful listening to find the

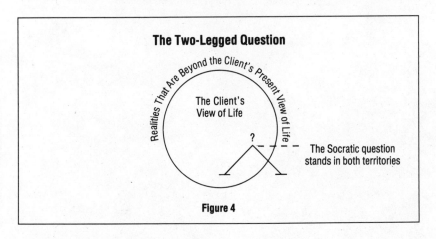

The Two-Legged Question

Realities That Are Beyond the Client's Present View of Life

The Client's View of Life

?

The Socratic question stands in both territories

Figure 4

circumference of the client's thought. If the question is entirely within the circumference, it will not have the stretching quality. If it is totally outside the client's thought, she will not be able to connect with it. The question needs to stand with one leg firmly in the client's way of looking at her world, and the other leg in new territory.

The question, "Why do you stand among the flowers and water the weeds?" is an example of the "two-legged question." The leg of this question that stands within the client's view has to do with weeds. The client was an expert in watering the weeds. The leg that stands outside her view has to do with flowers. She had not even noticed she was surrounded by beauty. The Socratic question begins with the client's view of life and gently invites the client to look up and respond to a fresh, new, accurate vision of reality.

CHAPTER TEN

PARADOXICAL INTENTION

MY FIRST ENCOUNTER with paradoxical intention occurred over forty years ago. I was the patient. During my high school days I had an eye twitch. This tic was sizeable and frequent enough to be noticeable to others, embarrassing to me, and worrisome to my parents. I don't know what caused it; there were probably many causes that teamed up to "help" me express my fear and anxiety in this way.

My brother, who had heard about paradoxical intention in a college psychology class, came home for a visit one weekend and talked with me. I well remember his instructions: "Take a little time each day to go to your room, look in the mirror, and make your eye twitch as many times as you can. Really work at it!" I decided to do it because I liked and respected him—and I was desperate.

So, later I went to my room, discreetly closed the door, and "practiced." I couldn't make it go! It was a real puzzler to me. I feared and hated that twitch. It came uncalled for at the most inconvenient times. Now I was actually summoning it and it refused to appear. This unexpected consequence kept me practicing. Then one day I noticed a smile in the mirror, and later my reflection laughed. The thought danced through my mind of the ridiculousness of what was happening. The tic disappeared when I laughed and has never returned.

It wasn't until later that I discovered paradoxical intention in my readings and realized the plan behind my brother's intervention. So I am indebted to him, his professor, and to Dr. Frankl for a lifetime freedom from a troublesome symptom.

The story is told of a robber knight who lived in medieval times. He was a terror! No one dared to challenge him. But one day he fell from his horse and his armor got caught in the saddle. To keep from falling, he grabbed the horse's tail and stumbled along in such a manner that everyone laughed. His power dissolved in their laughter. They were laughing at the foolishness of their own fears. Now they could resist and subdue him.[1] The power of paradoxical intention is a simple one: It helps clients laugh at and conquer the very thing that has been terrorizing them.

WHAT IS PARADOXICAL INTENTION?

The words "paradoxical intention" are important. It is paradoxical because one tries to make occur the very behavior one dreads. It is intentional because the client must *intend* the behavior, not merely think about doing it. In fact, anticipation only makes the behavior more likely to happen, such as, "I'm afraid I will cry," or "I'm going to cry."

Appropriate Use

As with any counseling method, one should give careful study and thought to this technique before using it. Also the counselor should avoid its use with a client who has endogenous depression (depression that is organically caused). Paradoxical intention was designed for use with conditions which are caused by anticipatory anxiety, not those which are biochemically caused. Obviously, one would not use it with a person who is suicidal, and it certainly would not be used in any way that would encourage sinful behavior.

Paradoxical intention is often the method of choice when counseling a client who is having involuntary reactions or responses because of fear or anticipatory anxiety. Logotherapists report the successful use of this method in the following situations: sweating,[2] compulsive handwashing,[3] compulsive hair-grooming in front of a mirror,[4] repeated lying,[5] fainting caused by fear of heights,[6] and staying home caused by the fear of crowded streets and buses.[7]

I have used this method with a number of client behaviors. One of these is crying. About ten years ago, a freshman student came to my office at the college the third or fourth day of the fall semester. She was desperately homesick. Her roommate, also homesick, had already moved out and gone home. Teri, now feeling even more alone, also wanted to go home. She said she thought she could stay if only she didn't cry when she left her room. She was skipping classes because she cried in her classrooms. Then she began to cry in my office.

I told her that I had an assignment that, if carried out, would help her. "Go back to your room and stand in front of the mirror and cry five times a day. Since you aren't going to many classes you will have plenty of time for this." Because students are somewhat used to having nonsensical assignments from their professors, she obediently went back to her residence hall and began the work. She came in the next day even more dejected. "I tried hard to cry and I could only do it three times." I explained that hard work and meeting assignments was a part of success in college and sent her back to work.

She came in the next day laughing and said, "This is crazy!" I agreed, and we had a great time laughing together. She was in a Christian campus group, for which I serve as faculty advisor, for four years. So I was able to be friends with her and to observe her growth from a shy girl to a poised servant leader in that group. My intervention that early September day

73

didn't cause this to happen, but I think it did help keep her on campus.

Long-term Attitudinal Change

At first glance, paradoxical intention appears to be a recipe-like intervention that deals only with behavior. This is not the case at all. There is a fundamental attitude change. As Frankl has noted, "This procedure consists in a reversal of the patient's attitude, inasmuch as his fear is replaced by a paradoxical wish. By this treatment, the wind is taken out of the sails of the anxiety."[8]

Elisabeth Lukas has also written about the permanence of this change: "In contrast to other techniques on the psychotherapy market, paradoxical intention brings about a change of inner attitudes, not temporarily but essentially a lasting new attitude toward oneself and one's feelings."[9]

Avoiding Deceit

I used paradoxical intention sparingly in the past because it has seemed to me to involve deceit. For example, I gave Teri an assignment to cry when I believed that it would do the opposite—actually help her stop her unwanted crying. However, for the last few years I have used it more often because I have learned that deceit does not have to be a part of the instructions. From the beginning, clients can understand the real purpose of the intervention through the use of humor and exaggeration by the counselor. The counselor can also explain directly that the goal is the reduction or disappearance of the symptom, but that the method will seem strange to the client.

Relaxation

I have become convinced by clinical observation that one of the reasons paradoxical intention works is that it relaxes people. It is clear to me from my teaching experience that relaxed learners learn most effectively. Tense, anxious learners can memorize until the test on Friday, but little genuine learning occurs. The same phenomenon may be seen in counseling. The relaxed client is less concerned with survival and more concerned with growth.

Paradoxical Intention and the Four Steps of Logotherapy

1. *Distancing from Symptoms.* In the situation with Teri, the homesick freshman, the use of paradoxical intention helped her laugh and relax. Her anticipatory anxiety ("I'll cry if I leave my room") was short-circuited by her relaxed emotional state. She thus distanced herself from the power of crying.

2. *Attitudinal Change.* Teri was able to achieve attitude transformation by realizing she was no longer the victim of unwanted crying just because she felt homesick. She was still able to cry in other situations when it was appropriate. She seemed released and more confident right away.

3. *Reduction of Symptoms.* As noted above, Teri's crying spells stopped. She could go to class without embarrassment.

4. *Reorientation to Meaning.* Because we were in a Christian campus group together we often talked about spiritual matters and about her meaning and mission in life. I did not stop working with her when the symptoms disappeared.

Cause and Effect?

Edith Weisskopf-Joelson, a professor at the University of Georgia prior to her death in 1983, took the position that we do not always have to find and eliminate the cause in order to relieve the client of the effect. "Although traditional psychotherapy has insisted that therapeutic practices have to be based on findings of etiology, it is possible that certain factors might cause neuroses during early childhood and that entirely different factors might relieve neuroses during adulthood."[10] According to Frankl, neuroses may have anticipatory anxiety as a primary pathogenic factor. There is something magnetic about that which we hate and fear. But if paradoxical intention can be applied so that the client ridicules his symptoms, *"the vicious circle is cut* and the symptom diminishes and finally atrophies."[11]

Understanding or Influencing the Self?

Most psychotherapies have as an important goal helping clients understand themselves. Logotherapy is more action-oriented. Attention is paid to *influencing* the self. If we find ourselves grumpy in the mornings, we can spend a great deal of time and energy trying to understand ourselves and how we got that way, or we can work to influence our behavior by paradoxical intention. "Good morning, grouch. . . . Go ahead and spoil my day. We'll see if you succeed! But put a little effort behind it, will you—it's no fun fighting a pushover."[12]

With phobic clients, the counselor can help the client to apply paradoxical intention. "Where in the world did I leave my fear today? It would be awful if I had lost it somewhere and couldn't find it anymore. It's been my steady companion for so long, I'd miss it terribly."[13] The place of humor and gentle ridicule may be seen in this application with fear and the previous one with grumpiness. As with the robber knight, whatever we laugh at cannot terrorize us. Humor comes naturally to logotherapy because logotherapy "recognizes a specifically human dimension oriented not toward pleasure and pain but toward sense (and nonsense). Sense and nonsense are the anchoring points on which humor is fastened like a balancing wire."[14]

The Child Client

Can paradoxical intention be applied with children? Carl Jepson, a dentist, has used this method to help children stop sucking their thumbs.[15] The parents are asked to stop reprimanding the child. The dentist then helps the parents establish thumb-sucking sessions on a daily basis for the child. These sessions are gradually reduced from the original length of ten minutes as the child desires. Each week the child sees the dentist "to discuss how this concentrated practicing is helping the child decide when he no longer needs thumb-sucking."[16] The child makes the decision to quit thumb-sucking, usually in two to eight weekly sessions. Jepson reported an 84 percent success rate. The treatment works with motivated children. As children get older, their motivation to stop usually increases.

James Yoder has reported a case study in considerable detail in which he effectively used paradoxical intention, applying Jepson's technique, with a seven-year-old girl.[17] He conducted three therapy sessions and one follow-up session with the girl.

Thumb-sucking practice sessions were established and carefully reduced in duration. The girl herself called Dr. Yoder when she decided to quit. He noted, "For the first time in her life she had slept an entire night without sucking her thumb."[18] More had happened than just the cessation of thumb-sucking. At the follow-up session, her mother said, "Stephanie has changed. She has matured."[19] The therapist treated the child with great respect. This was an important factor. Another factor in the success and growth was that "paradoxical intention as a technique was combined with human closeness and scientific detachment."[20] This is a powerful combination.

Incidentally, if you become very anxious about trips to the dentist, you may wish to apply Jepson's use of paradoxical intention with frightened patients. He urges such patients to exaggerate their fear and "be my best trembler, allow your knees to knock until I can hear them; or try to faint spectacularly. . . . That's how the wind can be taken out of the sails of your anxiety."[21] Thus the patient breaks the cycle of fear with a chuckle.

CHAPTER ELEVEN

DEREFLECTION

CHRISTOPHER MORLEY once said, "No man is lonely while eating spaghetti—it requires so much attention."[1] Concentration is obviously useful in life. But on what should we concentrate, the loneliness or the spaghetti? Perhaps there is a time for each. There has been an increasing emphasis the last twenty years on self-discovery and self-reflection. But self-reflection has been oversold. Socrates said that an unexamined life is not worth living. While this is probably true, it is also true that a life that consists *only* of self-examination isn't worth living either. Spending too much time thinking of oneself can cause a great deal of misery. Solomon in his twelve-chapter lament on meaninglessness (Ecclesiastes) is a case in point. If this book on self-reflection were the only book in the canon, we would be in bad shape. It reads, with a few exceptions, like one long sigh.

Hyperreflection, as noted by Frankl and other logotherapists, is excessive reflection on ourselves and our condition. Solomon talked about this: "All his days his work is pain and grief; even at night his mind does not rest. This too is meaningless" (Eccl. 2:23 NIV). Insomnia is usually caused by hyperreflection. Hyperreflection occurs when "I just can't get it out of my mind." "It" may be a predicament, a regret, or a fear, but usually the "it" is me. I am thinking too much of myself.

Hyperreflection can contribute not only to sleeplessness, but also to a number of other ailments, including some sexual dysfunctions, hypochondria, stuttering, test anxiety, depression, and fear of failure. Regarding stuttering, I know of a man in his fifties who has stuttered all his life. He is now a grandparent. He still stutters all the time with one exception—when he is playing and talking with his grandson, he talks normally. Children are great "dereflectors."

A Radically Different Method from the Usual Psychotherapy

Many, perhaps most counselors and psychotherapists focus primarily on the client's problem. There is a great deal of talk about it. This is a process of hyperreflection. Such a focus may actually deepen the client's anxiety. This has prompted several psychotherapists to discuss "Iatrogenic neurosis," a neurosis inadvertently caused by the physician or psychotherapist.

The first rule of the counselor should be "Do no harm." One way to do harm is to focus excessively on the problem. A counselor does need to listen to the client's story of suffering. The important thing is to move from the problem to treatment through dereflection at the appropriate time. Signals for the move could be when the client starts "circling," when the discussion is simply a "wallowing in the mire," when the client feels understood, or when the counselor has sufficient information to move to the treatment step.

Dereflection Applied in a Non-Counseling Setting

A number of years ago I was feeling behind schedule on a writing project. I was spending more of my time worrying about missing my self-imposed deadline than I was spending in productive writing. In replying to my concern, the wise editor said, "Don't get 'dis-eased' about 'dead lines.'" This one-liner enabled me to dereflect, stop worrying, and start writing. The editor knew I was conscientious and not just trying to escape from a responsibility. Dereflection would not have worked if I had been unmotivated.

Dereflection Applied with a Depressed Client

Karen had worked hard through a series of eight or ten counseling sessions to overcome her depression. We had tapered off on the frequency so that I was seeing her about once a month. The biggest barrier to her complete recovery was her brooding, or head trips back to her past. She was hyperreflecting on past events she regretted. It was my belief, and hers, that we had worked through the meaning of these past events sufficiently. It was perhaps a long-time habit that caused her to keep "sawing the sawdust."

So I asked her to think of long-time quests or dreams. She finally said that something she had always wanted to do was learn conversational French. When I asked why she had not done this, she said that she never had the time. Caring for her family and doing the other things she did made any personal learning time impossible. But she was spending about two or three hours a day (she said this was a conservative estimate) mentally rehashing the past. And she always felt more depressed after such brooding. After further Socratic dialogue, she bought a series of French language tapes. Then she began to develop an awareness of the "take off" for the head trip. Usually, when this occurred, she noticed that her concentration level on the task at hand was decreasing, or she was engaged in a repetitive task that did not use all her concentration skills. Then she would switch on her cassette recorder and use her time productively. The advantage of this learning program was that she not only dereflected, but she also felt better about herself with this new use of her time because she was fulfilling a life-long dream. In ways such as this we can teach our clients to "neglect" symptomatic behavior for a worthwhile activity.

The Use of Dereflection with Sexual Dysfunctioning Clients

Frankl used dereflection to treat a man for impotency as early as 1946. This was long before Masters and Johnson's work using the same goals of decreasing anticipatory anxiety and hyperreflection. Frankl reported in 1962 using dereflection with a woman who sought help to overcome her inability to experience orgasm.[2] Although she had been sexually abused by her father, that experience, traumatic as it was, was not causing her frigidity. She had been influenced by her reading of psychological articles to expect sexual neurosis because of her abuse. Frankl told her he could not begin treatment for two months. He told her she would be cured, but in the meantime she should attend to her husband's sexual pleasure. "Mrs. S. came back two days later, reporting she had experienced orgasm for the first time. Shifting attention from herself to her partner had resulted in the very thing she had prevented by her hyperintention and hyperreflection."[3]

Hyperintention means, in this situation, that the client's psychic energy is centered on the desire to experience an orgasm. There is no motivation to please the spouse because the client sees, and intends, only one goal. Whereas hyperintention is a single goal orientation, usually self-defeating, hyperreflection is the tendency to observe oneself. We become a spectator of our own actions and situations, and thus become insensitive to the needs of others. Suppose one spends all day thinking, "I'm a real louse. No one else is as stupid as I am." This hyperreflective, selfish behavior keeps that person from reaching out to another.

In helping clients with impotence or the ability to achieve orgasm, the counselor needs to work with both hyperintention as well as hyperreflection. If a husband wants to "prove himself" sexually, this hyperintention needs to be changed to a new intention—to satisfy his wife. In dereflection, the client is helped to stop hyperreflecting—to stop being a "spectator" of his or her sexual activity—and to focus rather on the pleasure of the spouse. Hyperintention and hyper-reflection are similar, but the former has to do with the will or purpose, and the latter has to do with attention—to what or whom are we attending?

The Application of Dereflection with an Anxious Student

Elisabeth Lukas reported working with a bright high school student suffering from test anxiety.[4] He was so upset that he developed psychosomatic stomach disorders. She asked his parents to avoid talking with him about school for three months. Instead they promoted more out-of-school activities such as soccer, electric trains, choir, and picnics. They talked with him about his accomplishments in these activities. They refused to commiserate with him about how bad school was. He became more involved with his activities and less anxious about school. His grades improved. The dereflection had been effective.

Dereflection and Logotherapy's Four Steps

Dereflection can often be used in each of the steps. With the first step—distancing from the symptoms—dereflection is often the method of choice. The symptoms are present and growing in severity because of the client's hyperreflection. Dereflection helps bring about the second step—change of attitudes—by providing a different point of view. As the client sees good things, he or she usually becomes more positive. The third step—the reduction or disappearance of symptoms—occurs as a matter of course. Thus only the fourth step—reorientation to meaning—remains. Dereflection will have helped in this step, but it will also be necessary to look with your client at goals and dreams and next steps before terminating the counseling.

Dereflection and the Reorientation to Meaning

A client came recently for his fourth, and what probably was his last counseling session. At least we decided to go to an "on call" arrangement rather than setting up any more sessions. He had been plagued by sleeplessness for many months, a reoccurrence of a similar ailment several years ago. He had, for a time, been taking tranquilizers prescribed by a psychiatrist. He stopped these because he was not alert enough to work. Now he was taking sleeping pills heavily but still was getting only a few hours sleep a night and was spending all his waking hours longing for sleep. His hyperreflection on sleep was lowering his effectiveness with people in his human service job, and was keeping him awake at night.

He had come for sessions every other week. This time interval is one I suggest for my clients unless there is an urgent crisis involved. It permits the client more time to do suggested tasks that come out of the counseling session. When I used to see most of my clients weekly, they would often come with no real work done related to their symptoms. Now clients are more likely to come with tasks done, and they are more highly motivated for the session. Also my suggesting every other week, except for crisis situations, tends to "decatastrophize" their situation and to let them know I do not see them as fragile. Of course, if I do not think they can "make it" that long, I see them in a week, or as needed. We worked the first session on some early childhood fears of failure that had been unexpectedly triggered. But it seemed to me that it was especially his dread of becoming a permanent insomniac that was making him depressed.

I asked that his wife come with him the second session. When I asked her what her main concern was for her husband, she said there were two. He spent too much time thinking of himself, and secondly, she was very concerned that he was getting dependent on the sleeping pills. During each of the sessions we worked with Socratic dialogue, dereflection, and paradoxical intention to take some of the dread from sleeplessness. He began to be released enough to take creative steps. He had stolen a cat nap at noon and another brief one after work. He stopped this practice. Then he started going to bed an hour later and getting up an hour earlier. Also if he woke up at 4:00 A.M. wide awake, he would get up. All these actions were helping to get his sleeping rhythm going again.

So his sleep was well enough in hand that he thought

he could handle it without more counseling. However, now he dreaded its recurrence. It had happened before, and it frightened him that it might happen again. At this point, I moved with him into the last step of counseling—helping him get reoriented to life with reduced symptoms. I told him, "Your biggest concern should not be how to avoid future attacks of insomnia because you cannot prevent them. Something may trigger your fears and the sleeplessness will return, or you may never have difficulty again. The important thing is not to spend time trying to figure out how to prevent recurring insomnia, but rather to be so well-prepared if it does come that it will not have a chance."

At that point I suggested several weapons to add to his arsenal. One was massage. Touch and massage are very relaxing activities. His wife could help him relax and sleep in this way. Humor was another resource we had not fully tapped. He has a sense of humor and wanted to learn more about it. I asked him to observe the funny happenings in his everyday life and to allow himself to laugh. Still a third way to overcome depression was with creativity. He said he used to do oil paintings but was no longer creative. I explained to him that working and playing in these areas would not only ready him for any future bouts with sleeplessness, but would make him a better dad, husband, and worker. As we talked about these different methods of combating sleeplessness and depression, he began to catch the vision. He said, "I'm getting so excited about trying these things that I don't know whether I'll be able to sleep tonight or not."

We both laughed at that. I had, of course, been utilizing dereflection as a method of helping him reduce his dread of another siege of sleeplessness. Obviously, the more he dreaded it, the more likely it was to happen. My effort was to get him to reflect away from the insomnia and on something manageable, namely building an armament so strong that he would become confident that he would survive and even win if it came to that.

The short number of sessions was an important factor in the counseling. As Lukas has noted, the high priority in counseling is to help clients find meaning. And once that meaning is found, their other problems may rapidly dissolve. Thus, as Lukas says, "Patients who can be helped in two or three counseling sessions, are not asked to come to fifty: This would only increase hyperreflection on their problems."[5] This, of course, is not true of all clients. Some will require many sessions to resolve their problems.

CHAPTER TWELVE

LOSS, GRIEF, AND EMPTINESS

THE FIRST THING I did with the family that came to see me was to ask to see the picture of the one who was *not* there. The mother took her billfold out of her purse, and from it took two pictures of her son—one of them was his senior picture. He was killed in an automobile accident a few months after he graduated from high school. Now, many months after the tragedy, they were seeking counseling because of the waves of sadness that would wash over them and immobilize them for a while. They were a close, loving family, so we did not have to deal with the distancing and old hurts that are sometimes present after such a tragedy.

The father, mother, and two remaining siblings had come—

an older brother, twenty, and an older sister, twenty-two. The boy who was killed in the accident had been very close to his two-year-old niece, the daughter of his sister. I asked to see the little girl's picture—she looked joyful and confident. I started to cry, and was puzzled why I was crying at that point. Then I understood, and told the family I was crying because I realized that the little girl would grow up without her uncle to love and enjoy her and that the uncle would also miss the special joy of that relationship. I had prayed before the family came that I might feel some of their sadness. And the prayer was answered at that moment. I believe Tournier is right: "The essential part of psychotherapy is listening, long and passionate listening, with love and respect and with a real effort at understanding."[1]

The father said he had not lost his faith, but he did spend a lot of time wondering why. I told him I thought it was a question he had to ask, but that I did not have an answer for it. I suggested he add another question to his thoughts: "How do I respond differently to life because of this son who lived eighteen years with us?" I made the suggestion for two reasons: First, I figured he would discover meaning not in an answer, but in his own *response* to his son's life. Second, giving people another question helps in the dereflection process.

About halfway through the session, we discovered a component of the tragedy with which they were all struggling. The boy had died before any family member could get to the hospital. They had not been able to say goodbye. This lack of closure added greatly to the meaninglessness of the tragedy. And yet as they talked, they began to discuss special interchanges the very day of his death which were deeper than the usual daily conversations. They found comfort in these observations. But we still have a lot of work to do. I recommended that they come back several times and told them the suffering might intensify before it lessens. I sensed some numbness in one or two family members, so I want to be available when this numbness, a natural sedative, wears off and the sharp pain is felt. Just recently another client entered my office and, after greeting me, said, "I have left shock and entered pain."

Significant loss naturally results in grief. And a sense of

meaninglessness often occurs as a part of that grief. It may have to do with the cause of the loss, such as the death of a loved one to the recklessness of a drunk driver. It may be a function of the timing of a loss, such as a little child or a teenager suddenly "cheated out of life." There may be other characteristics of the loss that are difficult or impossible to understand. In all these cases meaninglessness is a part of the grief.

Meaninglessness, however, takes the center stage in grief if the loss represents the *central value* in life. If a farmer loses his land by bankruptcy and if that land was "sacred" to him— more important than anything else, his natural grief will be prolonged and perhaps intensified by his view of a world devoid of meaning. The loss of a job may have a similar result, if it is similarly valued. If one's spouse dies and the remaining spouse sees no further reason to live, then the death of the surviving spouse is hastened. And most of us have observed that double tragedy. A chief value which is lost—a home, a spouse, a job, a friend—leaves the door open to illness, boredom, or irritation simply because life no longer appears to have meaning.

People are in a hierarchical value system. The chief value might be God, and the second, one's spouse or children, then siblings or close friends. But if God is given top value in our lives, then perhaps we might accept the loss of a loved one, and have to encounter the grief only, without the additional sense of meaninglessness. This was true of the above family. They have a deep faith. They are struggling with the question of meaninglessness because an accident, by definition, has no design or purpose. But in time they will turn from this focus on meaninglessness to dealing with the grief.

A Christian student came by my office at the college wanting to talk about how to help a friend who was suicidal. However, as we talked, the focus came back to the student herself. She had never understood why anyone would even entertain the thought of suicide. Now with the recent events in her own life, she knew why. She said, "I went through a time last week when I knew I was a burden on everyone, and I had no purpose in life." And for the first time in her life she briefly hosted the thought of suicide. In the last month she had a close friend die, her part-time work had gone sour, and she came back to college knowing she didn't have enough time to take care of all her commitments. As she continued to talk, she discovered that the *center* of her overwhelming sadness and meaninglessness was the death of her friend. She had not yet fully accepted his death. As the tears came, some of the denial crumbled. It was a painful, necessary step. Healing could not begin until she accepted the loss.

Children as a Resource

A pastor friend of mine has established a support group for spouses of people who have died of cancer. He reported a finding that surprised him. Many of the group members said that their adult children would not talk to them about the death of the loved one. The surviving spouses felt the need to talk about the loss, *especially* with their children. But, the pastor reported, there was another interesting development. The children's children felt very free to talk to a grandparent about the loss. They could share past happy events, talk about their sadness, and cry together. The grandchildren thus helped many surviving spouses to express their grief, accept their loss, and begin to live again.

Studying Our Own Death

In existential counseling, we bring ourselves, not just our methods, to the session. Therefore, if we are to work in counseling situations in which death is the central focus, we need to be sure we ourselves have faced that vision.

Love has great meaning because it is a connectedness. We are born with some kind of innate equipment that yearns for such a connection. An encounter with death severs the connection that has been established, forcing us to grapple with meaninglessness. What meaning can death have? What meaning can it have in our own lives? Martin Heidegger said that it is the vision of death that delivers us from the trivial cares of daily existence. The authentic life, he says, is "the life that is lived in the presence of death. . . . "[2] We are freed by the vision of death to commit our lives to tasks that matter.

Writing one's own obituary is a method often used to study

the prospect of one's death. Another often more effective method is to do a "fast forward" on our lives and think of our point of view on the last day of our lives. As we look back from that vantage point, we can determine what we should have been or done in order to experience a sense of fulfillment. Whatever that is, we then need to get on with it. As I worked through this exercise, I wrote about a page and a half of things I would have wanted to do or be. Putting my pen to paper in this way helped sharpen my vision of a meaningful future and resulted in the revelation of some specific goals I had not realized before.

One of my college students included the following paragraph in her Self-Directed Learning Project on loss and grief:

> I didn't know what to study for my SDLP. Then something happened in my life. For the last year, I have been working in a nursing home as an aide. In the first week I was there, three people died. I really didn't feel anything because I didn't know them. But after working for a while, I became attached to the residents, and this is what happened to me: About two months ago, a man died. He was always giving me a bad time and did not let me help him. In short, he was a nurse aide's nightmare. But this same man brought something into my life. Out of the blue he would say, "You're pretty!" or sing a song for me. The night he died, it finally hit me that I would never hear those things from him again. I felt that I had lost a part of myself that brought sunshine to my life.

Loss comes unexpectedly. Sometimes we miss even the abrasive things the person used to do. And each grief we experience comes with full power. Practice does not diminish a new grief. In the last sentence of the above statement, the student wrote, "I felt that I had lost a part of myself that brought sunshine to my life." A part of *ourselves* that we lose when we encounter grief is meaning. Therefore, as counselors we need to deal not only with grief but also with meaninglessness.

CHAPTER THIRTEEN

INTERVENTION WITH CANCER PATIENTS

HE POKED HIS HEAD in my office one afternoon and said, "I want to talk to you about my dying." Charles had been in one of my college classes five years ago. I remembered him because he was a self-motivated learner—the kind who does not say when he walks into a classroom, "What does the teacher want me to learn?" but rather, "What do I want to learn?"

Charles was now about twenty-five, battling cancer, and had learned from his doctor that he might not have more than six months to live. He said he came because he felt he had been "copping out" of life. Every day when he awoke, he asked himself, "Will what I'm planning to do today make any difference six months from now?" It didn't, so he wasn't doing anything. His wife, a sensitive, supportive woman, also felt that he was avoiding life.

My first question to him was, "When you learned from your doctor that your time was limited, which of your dreams were shattered?" He mentioned two. Later he told me of a third. The first was that he wanted to write and publish poetry. Although he once had penned a number of poems, he had now given up writing altogether. His second dream was to live in the Colorado Rockies. He had been there a number of times and loved that area. The third was that he wanted to teach. We talked that day about stained-glass windows and how sometimes small pieces of glass with the light shining through them are more beautiful than a window made of a large single pane. He decided to go after a small piece or two of his dreams, and made a commitment to resume writing poetry, and to bring a poem with him each week which we would go over together. He did this, and after a time I helped him submit a few of them to a publisher. They were not accepted, but he continued to write.

I asked him if he had ever shared with a group about what it meant to him to be going through this battle with cancer. He said no, but that he would think about it. Later he and his wife came to a class of advanced counseling students. He talked about life and about death. His wife shared what it meant to love someone and then see him so ill and in such pain. They both told the class to ask them any questions they wanted to. It was a lively discussion. One student said, "How can you talk about dying in the same tone as others might talk about going to the grocery store?" He replied simply, "Because I'm a Christian." It was a powerful witness. We were all crying by the time class was over. And I suddenly knew, and I think Charles knew, too, that he had become a teacher. He had taught more in an hour than most of us teach in years.

During this time with the class he had mentioned his love for the mountains. After class one of the students told Charles and his wife that they were welcome to use a cabin she and her husband owned in the Colorado Rockies. It was a great connection, and I hoped it would work.

Charles, however, got weaker and had to be admitted to the hospital. I visited him as often as I could until very near the end. His wife was able to be in the hospital around the clock and love and care for him. I attended his funeral and saw that another of his dreams had been realized. The memorial leaflet contained some of his poetry.

And his other dream? His body was buried high in the Rockies. Even now, many years later, I am moved by his love for life. When Moses and Elijah met with Jesus on the Mount of Transfiguration, Luke records that they talked about his exodus—his departure. When I think of Charles's departure and the witness of those last months, I am inspired to live whatever life is left with zest.

For the last twenty years or so, I have often asked clients the question, "What are your dreams?" A *goal* is practical and attainable. A *dream* looks impractical, but it has a lot of energy behind it. I've found most people from about age ten on are able, after thinking awhile, to identify one or two. I know they are getting there when they are a bit embarrassed to talk about it! That is the nature of a quest.

THE CONTRIBUTIONS OF LAWRENCE LESHAN

Lawrence LeShan, an experimental psychologist, has worked for most of his professional life as a compassionate psychotherapist and a careful researcher in a cancer service in a New York City hospital. The amazing story of his interventions with his patients, most of whom had been diagnosed as terminal, is told in the book, *You Can Fight for Your Life.*[1] Many of these patients were able to achieve long-term remission, some for five or ten years or longer. What has he discovered and how does he counsel?

LeShan's Findings

His first major finding was that the cancer patients with whom he had worked had lost their sense of purpose in life. There had been a relationship or a task that had been central in their lives, but when they discovered their illness, that purpose was lost. Another common factor was the loss of a parent or other emotional trauma early in life. A third factor was the patients' inability to express anger or hostility in their defense. They could be aggressive in standing up for the rights of others

93

but not themselves. Finally, they neither liked nor trusted themselves. They were alienated from themselves. From these last two factors came a basic emotion of despair.

LeShan discovered that, in some way, many of his cancer patients have had their energy output blocked. "The emotional force, like an inland pool that has neither fresh inlets nor outward flow, stagnates and becomes a kind of bog in which only the organisms of decay can find a home."[2]

LeShan's Psychotherapeutic Approach

It is up to the counselor to connect the patient with the refreshing streams of the outside world. Apparently all of us have cancer cells in our bodies most of the time but our immune systems keep destroying them. When the immune system shuts down, we are at risk. It is LeShan's (and many others') working hypothesis that one of the factors contributing to the shutdown is emotional stress. If this is true, the counselor is in an excellent position to help the patient get unblocked and "destressed."

LeShan describes himself as a crisis therapist who works like a gardener rather than a mechanic.[3] This metaphor speaks of life, respect, individualizing, and cultivating. These factors are needed because "those who were most completely in despair, who most thoroughly lost their sense of life's meaning, had the least resources."[4]

LeShan has often given Frankl's *Man's Search for Meaning* to his patients to read. He has found that they can connect the terror of the camps to that of their cancer. And they find hope in learning that Frankl made it.[5]

Although LeShan, as noted above, individualizes his work with each patient, " . . . the goal is always the same: to mobilize the resources of the total being in ways that will rekindle the creative life forces."[6] Patients have to be motivated to exert energy they don't seem to have. LeShan has found that the wish to live is a much stronger motivator than the fear of death.

Specific Techniques

LeShan uses a "time machine" technique whereby the patient is asked to think back to a specific time when he was a child.[7] Often this is a time of sadness and loss. The patient, with the therapist's help, can sometimes forgive or touch or hug that child, and thus can reconnect with an important part of himself.

I use a similar method, called "All of the River," in which I ask clients to think of their lives as a long river that is constricted with rough, white-water stretches in some places and has broad, peaceful stretches in others. The client talks about one of each of these times in his life. The idea is that we *are* all of the river and to rediscover meaning we need to be reconnected or reconciled with ourselves at any point in our past which we now view with anger, shame, or pity. And we need to be reminded of times of great joy we have experienced.

Another method that LeShan uses to get his patients moving is called the "first thing." He has found that most patients, because of their despair, have no goal for themselves. Therefore, he keeps asking them to voice a goal. One way he works at this is to say something like, "Everyone has a special song to sing. What is yours?" Once they have voiced a goal, he asks, "To accomplish that, what is the *first thing* you have to do?"[8] It has to be a single act and can be ever so small. But that act can be the beginning of a new life of hope.

HOSPICES

I recently completed two years as a hospice volunteer in our local hospital. The hospice movement, rapidly spreading throughout the country, helps dying persons and their families to live as fully as possible the last months of the patient's life. As a hospice volunteer, I sometimes visited patients, but my regular assignment was to lead a hospice support group. This group is comprised of the director, other hospice and oncology nurses, the chaplain, interns, and others.

During those two years I learned several things. One, a well-run hospice is an immeasurable resource for a community. Two, even an excellent hospice goes from one crisis to another. Three, there is a continuing need for new volunteers who can be trained and put to work. An additional lesson I learned was that hospice can be an effective community builder. Our local hospice organized a group of volunteers in an outlying small town who would visit a dying woman who lived alone. In the last months over thirty people were with her, each with a specifically assigned block of time each week. Later, one person from that community said that this had been a time when the community had become cohesive and been renewed.

THE RELATIONSHIP OF MEANING AND ALTRUISM

Irvin Yalom, a psychotherapist, has done a considerable amount of clinical work with persons dying of cancer. He reported that he observed repeatedly that "those patients who experience a deep sense of meaning in their lives appear to live more fully and to face death with less despair than those whose lives are devoid of meaning."[9] Yalom said that these patients had experienced several kinds of meaning but "none seemed more important than altruism."[10] He gave case studies of his patients to support this point of view. The common theme in the studies was the patients' strong desire, choice, and action to better the lives of others. One patient took as her last goal in life to humanize a very competent oncologist who appeared cold and uncaring. She expended great effort and succeeded in realizing her goal before the end of her life.

When we give to others we are altruistic. But there is an unexpected return. Altruism gives back to us meaning in life. We are back to Frankl's question: "What does life expect from us?" Joy and meaning are to be found not in personal pleasures, but in giving.

CHAPTER FOURTEEN

COUNSELING THE DEPRESSED PERSON FOR MEANING

As we have seen, Frankl has termed depression, addiction, and aggression the "mass neurotic triad."[1] It is his belief that feelings of futility, caused by an existential vacuum, contribute to each of the three disorders. In this chapter and the two that follow, some counseling approaches and methods will be described using meaning as the primary therapeutic factor in encountering this triad.

ENDOGENOUS DEPRESSION

Even endogenous (physically caused) depression can be approached by the logotherapy method of dereflection. It helps clients to know that they are not responsible for such cyclical depression. The idea is that they did nothing to get depressed;

therefore, they do not need to do anything to get over it. They are advised "to let the depression pass like a cloud over the sun."[2] Obviously, if there has been a diagnosis of endogenous depression, the client has seen a medical doctor, probably a psychiatrist, and is often under medication. A counselor can help such a client distance from some of the symptoms of depression by facilitating a change of attitude. The client can choose to take a courageous stand in the face of unavoidable suffering.

FUNCTIONAL DEPRESSION

What about those clients whose depression has no physical cause? Frankl has discussed the "unheard cry for meaning" which often results in depression, and sometimes in suicide.[3] Often people are in despair because of the loss of their greatest value—a family member or even a job. Their sense of loss goes beyond grief to depression because they have no other significant values; they are empty. Or they may not have suffered a loss. They simply haven't discovered anything worth living for. And they are tired of searching. Often people are seduced by the point of many television ads, namely, that the purpose of life is to find happiness in things. They are miserable, and therefore see life as meaningless and themselves as failures.

Distancing from symptoms is an all-important first step for the depressed client. The client is hyperreflected on his sad condition—a state of mind that sends him in downward spirals. The counselor needs to not only help the client get his mind *off* of his symptoms, but to get his mind *on* something that he *needs* to be thinking about.

Sleeplessness

Take sleeplessness as an example. Many depressed people report that insomnia is a part of their suffering. Sleeping pill companies are making millions because the insomniac hyperintends ("I will go to sleep") and hyperreflects (thinks about sleeping so much). Even the phrase "go to sleep" is an example of a false approach to the problem. We usually *intend* to go someplace.

Sleeping does not work that way. It is an involuntary act.

Therefore, people need to dereflect in order to sleep. Counting sheep is a popular acknowledgment of this truth. Also, the rhythm involved in sheep counting may help! It sometimes works because it is a distraction. A better way to sleep is to use the time for prayer, or to think on what is positive in our lives.

Philippians 4:4–8 NIV can be used as a prescription for those who suffer from sleeplessness. The directions could not be more suited for this ailment. "Rejoice in the Lord always. I will say it again: Rejoice!" (v. 4). This command requires dereflection. We take our minds off our predicament and center them on the Lord. We take our minds off our unhappiness and put them on joy.

"Do not be anxious about anything, but in everything, by prayer and petition, with thanksgiving, present your requests to God" (v. 6). Again we are directed to take the focus off the subject of our anxiety. The command to pray mentions thanksgiving, which is a positive experience, and an antidote to depression. Depression causes us to look down and in. Gratitude and praise to God cause us to look up and out. Thus, there is an enormous shift in viewpoint that occurs the instant the depressed person makes the choice to thank or praise God. When we look down, we see only limitations. We feel only guilt and despair and self-pity. When we look up, we sense God's unlimited resources. And we feel the acceptance and love of God. The counselor needs to challenge depressed clients to stop observing themselves and to start looking up. This act of faith can begin the healing process.

The next verse in the Philippians 4 passage talks about God's peace guarding our hearts and minds. "Finally, brothers, whatever is true, whatever is noble, whatever is right, whatever is pure, whatever is lovely, whatever is admirable—if anything is excellent or praiseworthy—think about such things" (v. 8). This verse is a great one for all anxious or depressed people, whether or not they suffer from sleeplessness. I have found the use of this verse, and the entire passage, useful in helping people dereflect.

There is an old Quaker saying, "Begin small and start promptly." This is a superior strategy to the depressed person's plan, "Begin big and start tomorrow." Therefore, the counselor can be helpful in building a strategy with the depressed client to make small changes.

The above approaches to sleeplessness help insomniacs lower their adrenalin levels. Archibald Hart has reported an estimate that fifty million Americans have difficulty sleeping.[4] It is his view that "for most of them, their sleeplessness will be caused by hyperarousal—they will be 'high' on too much adrenaline."[5] The stakes may be great in our work with sleepless clients. Hart believes that "excessive adrenaline production is the major cause of heart disease" and that "those who sleep poorly or insufficiently are at greatest risk for heart disease."[6] Therefore, our efforts to help insomniacs dereflect and sleep better may have far-reaching effects on their health.

Taking the Initiative with Depression

One of my clients was battling depression brought on by a series of unfortunate circumstances that occurred in her immediate family. She was not the cause of these adverse happenings, nor did she have any way of controlling them. But because there were several and they were close together, she fell into depression. It was holiday time and she was dreading seeing extended family members. Yet her home was viewed as the place to gather, and people often came without an invitation. She wrote me the following note about a small but significant step she had taken toward wellness. We had been talking in a previous counseling session about our freedom in every situation to choose our attitude toward that situation.

Our freedom to choose our own attitude is the most meaningful concept to emerge from our talks together. When I discovered I was to have uninvited guests for Thanksgiving weekend, I remembered we can choose our attitude—so I wrote and invited them. I discovered the small irritation (mostly due to the feeling that I have no control in this regard) disappeared and was replaced with one of anticipation. The weekend was extremely enjoyable for all.

This small act was a beginning in her becoming stronger. She had taken a first step toward getting back in control of her life.

Being Unhappy Does Not Mean That We Are Maladjusted

C. S. Lewis edited an excellent book, *Essays Presented to Charles Williams.* In it, he frequently noted the realism of Williams. Concerning happiness, Williams wrote, "The world is painful in any case: but it is quite unbearable if everyone gives us the idea that we are meant to be liking it."[7] Once the demand to be happy is withdrawn, we are relieved of a burden. And we need to be realistic about the sinful world we live in: "What is unforgivable if judged as a hotel may be very tolerable as a reformatory."[8]

A more realistic view is that we cannot avoid suffering, no matter how we live. Edith Weisskopf-Joelson noted that we should accept a certain amount of suffering and even give it a positive value.[9] The difficulty, she says, is that "our current mental-hygiene philosophy . . . stresses the idea that people ought to be happy, that unhappiness is a symptom of maladjustment."[10] This value system contributes to depression because "the burden of unavoidable unhappiness is increased by unhappiness about being unhappy."[11]

I have found clinically that *Christians* are often depressed about being depressed. This feeling is accompanied by a sense of shame at disgracing the name "Christian." So the counselor needs to help with guilt as well as depression. It is useful to suggest to such clients that they carefully read the stories of the Bible and note the full range of emotions that surged through believers. The Psalms document many negative emotional states that, when squarely faced, give way to gratitude and praise. The range in Psalm 77 TEV includes sleeplessness ("He keeps me awake all night," v. 4a), depression ("I am so worried that I cannot speak," v. 4b), accusing God ("Has he stopped loving us?" v. 8a), and hope ("You are the God who works miracles!" v. 14a).

The Use of Tests

The Purpose in Life Test (PIL), by James C. Crumbaugh and Leonard T. Maholick, is one which I have discovered to be useful with some depressed clients.[12] It consists of twenty questions which have to do with meaning. There is a brief manual available with this standardized test. The authors of the test caution against using it for diagnostic purposes without other corroborating evidences. I use it in my own counseling practice, not so much for diagnosing depression, but for generating and enhancing a Socratic dialogue about the search for meaning.

Dr. Crumbaugh has also constructed The Seeking of Noetic Goals Test (SONG),[13] which may be used in conjunction with the PIL test. The PIL test is an estimate of the degree of meaning one has found in life. The SONG test estimates the motivation one has to find meaning. If clients score low on the PIL and high on the SONG, it is Crumbaugh's view that the clients are good candidates for counseling. They lack meaning but they are motivated to discover it.

Depression as a Valuable Symptom

Pain alerts us that some part of our body needs attention. In a similar manner, depression may make us aware that we need to deal with a lack of meaning in our lives. Therefore, depression can serve a purpose and have a meaning. It can force us to deal with boredom and with a life without clear goals. Clients make their way out of depression by beginning to make choices, no matter how small, and to act on them.

CHAPTER FIFTEEN

VIOLENCE AND MEANING

AGGRESSION IS INCLUDED with depression and addiction as part of the "mass neurotic triad." But at first glance, aggression seems to be in a class by itself. Persons who are depressed and addicted may be seen as "doing it to themselves," whereas the aggressive person is violent with others. Underneath, the three characteristics have some similarities. There is damage being inflicted, either on self or others, usually both, in each disorder. Counselors observe in all three that the person seems to be out of control.

POWERLESSNESS

Rollo May has studied the roots of violence. He has concluded that "violence has its breeding ground in impotence and apathy."[1] These two characteristics—impotency and apathy—sound very much like the futility of the mass neurotic triad.[2] May's point is that a state of powerlessness causes the apathy which triggers the violence. He quotes Edgar Friedenberg: "All weakness tends to corrupt, and impotency corrupts absolutely."[3]

I have seen what May is talking about. Today a woman came for counseling and told the story of her five-year marriage. She grew up with a passive mother and a domineering, drinking father. She married a domineering, drinking man and has been a passive wife. She had been so passive that whenever her husband was upset with her, she apologized whether she thought she was in the wrong or not. Finally, this last weekend she stood up for herself, and he beat her up. He was cowardly, and felt powerless to work it out verbally. He lacked impulse control, so he used his hands.

DESPAIR

May has written a little book, *The Courage to Create*, in which he talks about despair.[4] This is a significant topic because the mass neurotic triad—depression, aggression, and addiction—all have despair as their common denominator. He points the way to treatment for violence. We need to help the violent person gain courage. May notes that the existentialists have proclaimed that "courage is not the absence of despair; it is, rather, the capacity to move ahead *in spite of despair.*"[5]

Paul Tournier also has detected that violence is rooted in meaninglessness and despair. His book, *The Violence Within*, is a major contribution to an understanding of this dark side of all of us.[6] He quotes philosopher Georges Gusdorf: "Violence is the opposite of strength, for the energy it brings to bear is only the energy of despair."[7] Tournier also notes that the root of violence is the problem of evil. Even though the need to love is a part of us all, it is not the only part. "What I am maintaining here is that there is also, and at the same time, in the same heart, a need to hate and to kill."[8] This truth helps us as counselors to recognize what we are up against. Violence is no easy adversary.

As counselors how do we work with violent clients? I've

found it's easier to work with them than it is to get them into my office for counseling. Usually, as in the situation above, it is the battered wife who comes in, or the spouse whose mate is abusing the children. We need to connect the abused person with a network of helping people. This may include a shelter for women and children, social services, a lawyer, or police. Assaulting is, after all, against the law. Marriage is sacred, but so is life.

If it is the usual situation of a husband who has been violent with his wife, and if she elects to stay with him, I try to see to what extent she is held "psychological hostage." Is she staying because she is afraid to go? If her decision to stay seems to be a considered one, I ask her to bring her husband with her. Violent men are usually frightened by the prospect of being left alone. The violent person, as noted above, is short of courage. Therefore, they will often be motivated to come. After one session the counselor can probably tell what the prospects are for change. Some cities have groups for battering men, and for couples in which one or both is hitting the other. A referral to one of these groups may be useful. Social service or the victim witness unit of your police department can often tell you if such groups are available.

Daniel Sonkin and Michael Durphy have co-authored a workbook which I have found quite helpful. Their basic assumption agrees with what I have seen clinically: "Many men who batter feel out of control in their lives."[9] They note that their underlying purpose in working with violent clients is "developing a sense of personal power without taking power away from others."[10]

One couple I counseled had been hitting each other for six years. Both had little anger control, but the woman was at much greater risk because she was smaller and not as strong. The husband also drank occasionally. Knowing the statistics ("in 60 to 80 percent of the battering incidents, the batterer . . . is under the influence of alcohol or other drugs"[11]), I asked the woman how often he had been drinking when he hit her. She replied, "About three-fourths of the time." So I recommended that he go as a first step in our work to a professional alcoholism counselor I knew. He did, and he was told that he was on the edge of becoming an alcoholic. He was at risk every time he drank. This helped because it gave him new information.

Next I required a commitment from them never to even touch each other when they were angry for as long as we worked together in counseling. Then I introduced "time-out" as the major way to regain control of their impulses. Persons who lack anger control are taught to say, "I'm beginning to feel angry, and I'm going to take a time-out."[12] This is a powerful statement because it calls for awareness and non-violent action. The counselor, with the spouse's help, needs to help the client discover clues to rising anger, such as increased physical movement, flushing of the face, clenched fists, pointed finger, or loud voice. The angry person says when he will be back (usually a half-hour or hour), then leaves. Physical exercise, such as walking, is encouraged. Drinking and driving are forbidden during the time-out. The procedure needs to be followed very closely, including *practicing* time-outs before they are actually needed.

I found out when this couple fought (10:00 P.M. to midnight) and asked them to disagree at other times, not at that time. I asked where their battlefield was (the kitchen), and instructed them to always have their disagreements in other parts of the house. Also I asked them to *sit* during their arguments, out of arm's reach of each other.

While all this was going on, I was teaching the couple how to talk with their mouths instead of their hands. They did love each other, and they were willing to work hard. Once in a while I used humor, "Of course you love each other; why else would you have hit each other for so many years?" The violent person needs to learn to laugh, and particularly to laugh at himself.

Another front we worked on was their spiritual lives. What was their relationship with God? What was their understanding about forgiveness? What had meaning for them in life—excited them? What was life asking of them?

After this plan was enacted, there were no incidents of hitting reported by either spouse. There were a number of time-outs taken. This increased the feeling of control of the one who took the time-out, and increased the trust of the other person. After about eight sessions, we tapered off from weekly sessions to every other week, then a session a month, and finally to an "on-call" arrangement. They did not call me for emergency counseling, but they did call about a year later to let me know they were doing well.

Now I could have related a failure story instead of this success story, but it wouldn't have been as illustrative! The point I wanted to make is that the counselor needs to work on several fronts at once, including the stopping of violence, the teaching and practice of communication skills, and the discussion of spiritual values. Felt success because of solid accomplishments on all fronts can help violent persons increase their courage and sense of personal power so they will be more likely to make non-violent choices in the future.

TEACHING GENTLENESS AS A WAY OF LIFE

At the same time that I am working with individuals, couples, and families on anger control, I am talking with them about something *not* on the dark side of their lives. We cannot empty lives of violence without filling them with something else. I therefore talk with clients about the meaning of a gentle lifestyle in a violent world.

My father was a gentle man. He knew he was a man, so he didn't feel the need to prove it to himself or to anyone else. Someone has said that "only the strong can be gentle, and only the gentle can be strong." The gentleness that I learned from my father has sometimes been mistaken for weakness, but that is part of the risk of choosing gentleness as a way of life.

Gentleness means positive ways of relating to others rather than being physically and verbally violent. "Physical violence" is self-explanatory. "Verbal violence" includes sarcasm, name-calling, teasing (if it's fun for the teaser but not the teasee), and yelling.

The violent nature of yelling is often underestimated. Some elementary school teachers in one of my classes asked their students what they would like their parents to stop doing. The number one response from first through sixth graders was yelling. Children live in a world of giants. If we looked up and saw a twelve-foot giant screaming at us, we would probably tremble and view the episode as violent. As Tournier noted concerning violence, "Few parents actually realize the impression they make on their children, because in their children's eyes they are all-powerful."[13] There is another reason why children fear yelling. Since several behaviors actually escalate violence instead of decrease it, such as yelling and slamming doors, children who are yelled at know that worse violence often follows.

Teaching Clients What Gentleness Is

One way to help clients become gentle is to teach them what gentleness is. I try to communicate the following ideas as we talk together about alternatives to a violent way of life. I focus especially, but not exclusively, on families.

Gentleness is being as concerned with kindness as we are with honesty. In a beautiful little book about reconciliation, *Treat Me Easy*, Earnest Larsen says, "It is impossible to be too honest; but it is very possible to be honest without being kind. *I'm sorry; I've got to call a spade a spade* is the creed of some so-called honest people. But more often than not this means, in the name of honesty I will punish you."[14]

Gentleness is adopting the point of view, "Catch them being good." We all know the feeling of being caught when we've been doing something bad. But how many of us remember being caught when we were doing something good? It is one of life's serendipities to be caught in such circumstances. A little recognition goes a long way. Statements such as, "Hey, you're doing a good job on that!" or "I want you to know I'm really proud of you," serve to build strength in those we love.

Gentleness is confronting others when they need it. We all need confronting at times. Others can hear our confrontations better if our voices are kept low and calm. Some may object and say this means we will have to pull our punches. Another way to look at it, instead of using a fighting image, is to see two persons standing face-to-face, one with his or her hands on the other's shoulders, saying what needs to be said. There is no loss of directness, but rather the addition of gentleness.

Gentleness is not excusing a "short temper" as something

that can't be helped. Henry Drummond, in his commentary on 1 Corinthians 13, *The Greatest Thing in the World*, has some helpful reminders: "No form of vice, not worldliness, not greed of gold, not drunkenness itself, does more to unChristianize society than evil temper. For embittering life, for breaking up communities, for destroying the most sacred relationships, for devastating homes, for withering up men and women, for taking the bloom of childhood, in short, for sheer gratuitous misery-producing power, this influence stands alone."[15]

Gentleness is gained by studying the life of Christ as reported in the gospels, and learning from his gentle lifestyle. Two friends of mine and I met together every Friday morning for nearly two years to study the life of Christ and to consider the implications of that life for our own lives. I nearly always left these meetings with an awareness of having been in the presence of the Lord.[16] "Come to me, all of you who are tired from carrying heavy loads, and I will give you rest. Take my yoke and put it on you, and learn from me, because I am gentle and humble in spirit; and you will find rest. For the yoke I will give you is easy, and the load I will put on you is light" (Matt. 11:28–30 TEV).

CHAPTER SIXTEEN

ADDICTION AND MEANING

SOME ADDICTS USE drugs to slow down while others use them to speed up and brighten their lives. Some addicts even use them for both purposes in a single day. This kind of use or abuse has prompted Elisabeth Lukas to make the following insightful statement: "The desire for a quick change in activity level, regardless in what direction, is now considered a decisive component in addiction."[1] The "quick fix" from suffering on the one hand and boredom (a kind of suffering) on the other is a clear requirement of the alcoholic or other kind of substance abuser. And yet addicts seek more than a quick fix.

JOINING THE ADDICT

We as counselors cannot be useful to addicts unless we connect with them in some positive way. The strongest connection we can have with them is a spiritual one. William James said of alcohol, "Not through mere perversity do men run after it. . . . The drunken consciousness is one bit of the mystical consciousness." [2]

Why do most people laugh at nonviolent drunken behavior? Could it be that the "released," joyful behavior is funny, even inviting? The intoxication caused by alcohol and the exuberant result of the Holy Spirit's presence were confused even at Pentecost (see Acts 2).

The alcoholic seeks to move from despair to joy, but instead moves to a numbed condition, and from there to deeper despair.

We can join the alcoholic in his or her spiritual quest. This is the point of connection for Alcoholics Anonymous, and it shows respect for the one who is addicted. He or she is not just a pleasure-driven hedonist. Holmes has accurately pointed out that if we really were dominated only by the desire for pleasure "there would be little hope the alcoholic would suspend the pleasure of perpetual intoxication for the agony of sobriety." [3] Often, the recovering alcoholic trades temporary pleasure for agony because of the drive for meaning.

The alcoholic's immediate thirst, however, is not for meaning, but rather for another drink. That is why a treatment center which utilizes many methods (including depriving the addict of alcohol) is usually more effective than the individual counselor in the recovery process.

GETTING THE ALCOHOLIC TO TREATMENT

When I work with families struggling with substance abuse, I refer the suspected addict to a professional alcohol or drug counselor for an evaluation. The counselor administers some tests, does a personal and family history, and conducts an in-depth interview. A little later, the counselor does a follow-up session with the client in which the findings are communicated. I have found that a professional alcoholism counselor, for example, can bring added influence to a referral for treatment. And the experience can be a somewhat sobering one for the problem drinker who has not yet reached the alcoholic stage. If the counselor's evaluation recommends treatment, then I put my weight behind the rest of the family to get that person into treatment as quickly as possible. In addition to in-patient treatment, some cities have evening treatment programs which permit people to keep their jobs, and which eliminate the difficult re-entry phase following treatment.

THE MEANING OF A PLANNED INTERVENTION

When the false meaning of the moment—the addiction—continues to have greater significance than the long-term meaning, then it is time to seek the services of the professional alcohol counselor again. Such a counselor will usually help family members and very close friends plan and practice an intervention. Then, at a time arranged by the person closest to the alcoholic—usually the spouse—the group confronts the alcoholic while he is sober. In a recent planned intervention, the assembled group confronted the alcoholic on his way to the bathroom first thing in the morning. He was, of course, quite vulnerable. Each family member, in a way that had been orchestrated by the counselor, told the alcoholic specifically how his drinking had hurt them. Each one asked him to go get treatment. The counselor was also present to prevent arguments and power struggles. The alcoholic chose to go to treatment that very day. He could defend and deny with one family member at a time, but the caring confrontation of this total group of people who loved him made sense to him, and he dropped his defenses.

MOTIVATION

James Crumbaugh has had many years of experience in applying logotherapy methods to alcoholics in a Veterans Administration Medical Center.[4] I have found his five-step method useful in understanding the recovery process of persons suffering from any addiction:

1. Choosing a basic belief about the nature of the world, either the mechanistic view or the teleological view. (It is Crumbaugh's empirical judgment that about 80 percent to 90 percent of alcoholics adopt the teleological—there is an ultimate purpose—view of the world.)

2. Building self-confidence.
3. Stimulating creative thinking.
4. Establishing deep interpersonal relationships.
5. Finding a task or life activity, e.g., a vocation, or a cause to believe in.[5]

How does a counselor help clients take these five steps? Whenever beliefs, creative thinking, and choices are involved (as in 1, 3, and 5, above) Socratic questioning is valuable. Such questions cause the client to take a fresh look at his or her belief system and opportunities. Building self-confidence and establishing deep relationships (2 and 4, above) are at least partially the results of the counselor's time investment and belief in the client.

This five-step process leads into the spiritual dimension of life. The last two steps, especially, gently refocus the alcoholic's mind off of self, which led to the despair and addiction in the first place, and on to the needs of others, the first major move toward wellness. The Christian faith offers deep personal relationships and a cause in which to invest.

INTERVENING WITH CO-DEPENDENTS

An important pathway to meaning is through connectedness, especially close connections with family, friends, classmates, and co-workers. This route to meaning is usually denied to the family of the addict. The alcoholic's family members, the co-dependents, learn not to trust others. And since trust is the basis of all good relationships, the co-dependents live in meaningless isolation. The addict's spouse is caught up in covering for the addict, or in anger, in grief, or in the never-ending work of providing for the welfare of the children.

In a real sense, all the family members of the alcoholic are co-dependents. However, this term is usually reserved for the spouse. The co-dependent spouse who comes for counseling needs help in many areas. Chief among these is accepting reality. The co-dependent's lifestyle is characterized by denial and dishonesty, just as the alcoholic's is. A Socratic question for a co-dependent might be, "As you look at your family, what do you see?" A similar question that adds the dimension of distancing might be, "If you could see your family as a neighbor or close friend sees it, what would you see?" These questions call for a vision of reality.

Anne Wilson Schaef has noted that "an addiction is anything we feel we have to lie about."[6] She points out that, after we help co-dependents extricate themselves from the web of co-dependency, we need to be aware of behavior that triggers a reinmeshment. These include dishonesty, not taking responsibility, self-neglect, manipulation, and comparison of self with others.[7]

Only those who have lived with an addict can understand the unpredictability and chaos that is a part of daily life. The quest is not for meaning but for survival. The best-laid plans of the morning are swept away in a drunken evening. A counselor's most important skill in attempting to intervene with the family of an addict is networking. The needs of a family in such a crisis are too overwhelming for Lone Ranger ventures. Thus, a network of friends, family, and professionals on whom the family can rely is vital. The pastor or other counselor needs to be on a first-name basis with school counselors, social workers, alcohol counselors, and other professionals. A rule for survival in such intervention is, "Don't go down in a deep well without a long rope." So the networking is not only valuable for the addict and family; it also is important for the mental health of the counselor.

Adult Children of Alcoholics

There are many adults who are only partially functioning in their jobs, their marriages, and their other obligations and opportunities. The cause of their poor performance and lack of meaning in life is not apparent. Often, alcohol is not suspected because it is not in the immediate picture. But look again; if it is not in the foreground, it is often in the background.

These adults are caught up in anger, guilt, fear and futility because they grew up the children of alcoholics. As children they learned to not talk about their feelings and to not rock the boat. These learnings set them up for intense difficulties in their future family and work roles. The walls they built to provide safety as children have continued to insulate them from reality and close relationships through adolescence and adulthood, and will continue to do so unless they receive help.

In the first session with these clients, I inquire about their family story. If they are the adult children of an alcoholic (COA), I attempt to make a referral to a COA group. In such a group they can begin to get reconnected with others by discovering that their situation was not unique. They are no longer alone. They are then able to make sense of their past and their present as they learn the dynamics of an alcoholic family. And they can begin to deal with their legacy of not talking and not trusting.

There are millions of COA's, but they don't meet us in church, at work, or in the counseling office with a name tag that says "COA." It is up to us to be aware of their isolation and lack of meaning that can sensitize us to the nature of their problem.

CHAPTER SEVENTEEN

GUILT, GRACE, AND MEANING

I RANG A DOORBELL in the apartment complex with one part of me wanting a response and another part of me hoping nobody was home. A man named Tim had called me to ask if I would come over to talk about "some spiritual matters." I had never met him. He said he had been in a workshop once that I had led, and he went on to say that he was dying of cancer. As I stood outside the door, I heard a call, barely audible, "Come in."

Tim was sitting by a desk breathing through an oxygen tube that was attached to a noisy compressor in the next room. He motioned me to sit down in a nearby chair, carefully saving his breath whenever a gesture would do as well. Tim said he wanted to talk about getting ready to meet God. He was about fifty years old, and had been employed in a retail business before his illness made working impossible. He knew he didn't have much time left.

I asked him to show me how God would look if he had a human form and was looking at Tim now. Tim stood up with great effort, folded his arms, looked at his wrist watch while looking down, tapped his foot, and said, "When are you going to get your act together?" Then I understood his desperateness—he had to get his act together with almost no time to look at a script or to practice. We talked some more to help me understand his spiritual needs. Then I talked with him about guilt, and about the grace of God and the love of Jesus. He did not seem to be focused on a particular sin, yet he felt very distanced from God and unready to die. I suggested that another way to view God would be to see him with arms outstretched willing to forgive, and inviting Tim to experience his love. Tim was getting noticeably weaker and needed to rest, so I left after telling him I would be glad to come back if he wished. He had a support system of people who came by regularly, and he had two other people he was talking to about deep concerns. I left feeling empty and ineffective. Tim died two weeks later. I never knew whether I was useful to him or not. A mutual friend told me he did not bring up spiritual concerns again after my visit, but this information also left me feeling ambivalent.

I have asked many people to define their image of God. Most have taken Tim's stance, suggesting condemnation or accusation. Quite a few have had God wagging a finger at them. This is tragic because the New Testament presents *Satan* as the accuser, not *God.* William D. Eisenhower has discussed this fear and guilt which so many people experience. He says, "What purposes does it (fear) serve? The first has to do with meaning, the second with morality. The fear of God makes life meaningful."[1]

Eisenhower argues that the fear of God is meaningful because fear is the beginning point of the faith journey. It is fear that brings us to a kneeling posture before God. Moses was afraid as he stood before the burning bush. The shepherds were frightened by the angelic choir. Paul was scared on the road to

Damascus. "Only fear of the Lord gives to life the meaning that makes love possible," Eisenhower says.[2]

He goes on to say that fear is one of the chief motivations for morality. We obey God for a number of reasons, one of which is fear. I agree that the fear of God should be taken seriously. Jesus himself said "Do not be afraid of those who kill the body but cannot kill the soul. Rather, be afraid of the one who can destroy both soul and body in hell" (Matt. 10:28).

Paul Tournier has noted that guilt is universal. The important thing is whether it is repressed or recognized. If guilt is repressed, then the results are fear, anxiety, anger, aggressiveness, and a lack of awareness of one's faults. "But consciously recognized," Tournier says, "it leads to repentance, to the peace and security of divine pardon, . . . and a steady weakening of aggressive impulses."[3]

It is important for a counselor to accept rather than judge. There is only One who is qualified for the complicated task of judging. A part of accepting is to hear what often amounts to a confession. Tournier has written about the powerful effect of confessing. "Very often it is not only the decisive religious experience of freedom from guilt, but . . . the sudden cure of a physical or psychological illness."[4]

Tournier has made the point that false and true guilt are closely intertwined. The counselor again needs to be careful on passing judgment about what part of the guilt is true and what is false. It is all *felt*, and that is the important point. Donald Tweedie has summarized well the distinction between true and false guilt, and its implications for counseling. He noted that true guilt is an act of grace. God judges us through our conscience. But false guilt comes from other people's judgments. It is a great burden. "The therapist is, of course, not able to discriminate between these two in most cases, nor fortunately, is it his task to do so," Tweedie says. "However, he must deal with them both as components of the personal despair of his patients."[5]

LOGOTHERAPY AND GUILT

A strand that runs from Frankl's first writings to Lukas's present ones is the theme of *restitution*. We discover meaning in our guilt-suffering by doing what we can to help the person injured by us. Elisabeth Lukas presents a case study in her treatment of a woman who was guilty of wrongs to her husband and son.[6] As she made voluntary sacrifices for each of them, she was able to increase the quality of their lives and lessen her own felt guilt.

Making restitution is not only a logotherapy concept, it is a Christian duty. The Christian therapist who is grounded in biblical revelation "must, in reference to this revelation, go beyond the logotherapeutic teachings in order to satisfy the responsibility entailed in a biblical vocation."[7] This "going beyond" involves the counselor in the biblical concept of grace.

GRACE

Michel Quoist's moving book, *Prayers,* contains a poem-prayer that describes the power of guilt—and of grace. Most of the prayer is from the viewpoint of the "pray-er" who has selected the sin "the way a customer makes his purchase." He finds that the sin will not let him go, and he is ashamed and discouraged. At the end of the prayer God responds saying that it is vanity that keeps him down. And then these last four amazing lines:

> Ask my pardon
> And get up quickly.
> You see, it's not falling that is the worst,
> But staying on the ground.[8]

I have come to believe that this is true in my own life. It is pride that keeps me from receiving grace. I am looking down, flat on my face or slogging along engrossed in myself and my guilt, instead of looking up, joyfully receiving God's grace, and then running and leaping with the new freedom.

Looking Up

How do we help others stop looking down and start looking up? One way is by a more-or-less spontaneous act of human grace. It may be a touch, a small gift, a phone call, or listening. We need to *connect* with them in some way. A gracious act, done in love, reconnects them with life by pulling them out of their quagmire of self-pitying isolation. In a counseling session it can be an affirmation, a mention of an event that occurred in the client's "better days," listening intently to a confession, or crying with the client.

Grace as a Gift

All of the above acts are little gifts that we give the client. Grace and gift are closely allied concepts in the New Testament, with the Greek word *charis* tying them together. W. E. Vine noted that concerning grace in the New Testament,

> . . . there is stress on its freedom and universality, its spontaneous character, as in the case of God's redemptive mercy, and the pleasure or joy He designs for the recipient; thus it is set in contrast with debt, Rom. 4:4, 16, with works, 11:6, and with law, John 1:17.[9]

Grace Is Not Imposing Guilt

It is an act of grace not to lay guilt on others, whether they are clients or others that we encounter in our day. During the first two weeks of last semester, I noticed that a student was sleeping some in one of my college classes. She was obviously *trying* to stay awake. But her full-time job and her studies didn't leave enough time for sleep. I tried to think of a creative approach that would not add to the guilt she was already feeling. Then one day I asked her to stay a moment after class, and told her that I could tell she was trying hard to stay awake. Then I thanked her for coming to class every day rather than staying home once in a while to sleep. She was wide-awake for the rest of the semester. After the semester ended, she wrote me a note to say that she had learned a great deal in the class, and

> . . . the one thing I feel I learned the absolute most from was when you took me aside one day after class and told me how you had noticed how tired I always was during class. I thought for sure when you mentioned it that I was going to be in a lot of trouble. But instead you took a

different approach, and thanked me for coming to class. I think because of the approach you took from then on I tried to stay very alert in class. It taught me that I should always look to the bright side of a problem. Instead of reprimanding someone for the wrong they have done, I should try to find something positive about it if I can.

This student plans to be a teacher. One of the exciting things about a little act of grace such as this is that it has the potential of being replicated sometime in the future.

LETTING GO

All of the above definitions of grace echo the idea of gift-giving. But people can't receive a gift if their hands are fists, angry and hanging onto their guilt and fear. As Henri Nouwen has said, "*When you dare to let go and surrender one* of these many fears, your hand relaxes and your palms spread out in a gesture of receiving."[10] This is a clue that suggests we also need to hear and deal with our clients' fears before they can relax and receive the gift of God's grace. Once in a while I've found it useful to ask clients to "three-dimensionalize" the process of letting go. I ask them to close their hands into fists, visualizing the fear onto which they are hanging, then to gradually open their fists, letting go of that fear.

A friend of mine told me an interesting story about hanging on to guilt. Ten years ago he was in a work situation in which he was very unkind to a fellow employee. He was frustrated with his job, and his co-worker became the focal point of all these frustrations for two or three months before he left the job and moved to another city. He often thought about his meanness to her, and the guilt continued to grow. Finally, after nearly ten years he went back to the city, looked her up, and talked with her. She was glad to see him! He told her of the growing guilt he had felt all these years, and also related how he recalled treating her so badly. She couldn't even recall those last months and his mistreatment of her ten years before, even though the memories of his misconduct had haunted my friend all that time. He couldn't forget, and she couldn't remember!

Receiving Grace for Our Guilt as a Counselor

I have finished many counseling sessions only to be smitten with guilt at the moment or to have it creep up on me during the night. Some typical thoughts have been, "Why did I say that?" or "Why didn't I say that?" or "I took too much responsibility for the session," or "I didn't take enough responsibility." Talk about true or false guilt! Who can separate the counselor's guilt into these two categories? After my visit with Tim, mentioned at the beginning of this chapter, I felt guilty because there were no evidences that I had been useful.

What have I done about the guilt? I have sought to become more competent through the occasional use of co-therapists when I work with couples and families, attending workshops in counseling areas in which I feel weak, reading widely, and discussing cases confidentially with peers (a practice that is ethically sound). These steps have helped, but they have not eliminated all the surges of guilt. I pray for the family, couples, or individual with whom I've counseled and commit them to the Lord. In fact, I usually pray for myself as a counselor before the session and for the client after the session. Then, I confess to God what I believe I erred in doing or not doing, and receive his grace and forgiveness. I do that when I am at my best spiritually. At other times I fail to commit it to the Lord, and I toss and turn all night.

There are some who say we should not spend time and energy thinking about our clients. The responsibility for their lives is theirs, not the counselor's. That is true. I don't want to take their responsibility away from them. But I have not found a way to care about them at 4:00 P.M. and not care about them at 10:00 P.M. Thank God for grace!

True guilt is a gracious act of God. We can utilize guilt to help us troubleshoot our moral condition in the same way that we localize physical pain to determine what is wrong with our body. Guilt gives us a second chance to right our wrongs. God's way of dealing with us is gracious, even though it may not always appear so.

CHAPTER EIGHTEEN

SUFFERING—PAIN OR MISERY?

CLIENTS USUALLY COME to a counselor because they are suffering. And although the counselor may or may not be able to help them become free of pain, the first step will be to understand the suffering and try to localize the pain. Our job is to find the center of the psychic or spiritual suffering and its cause.

DISCOVERING THE REAL NATURE OF THE SUFFERING

A third-grade boy was stealing lunch money at school. His parents brought him and their other children to my office because I told them I preferred to work with total families when a child is in trouble. The family member who is in trouble or who is the most troubled is called the "identified client" (IC) in family therapy literature. The boy, of course, was the IC.

123

When a child is the family's IC, the first question I ask myself is a family systems question: "How is this child trying to save the family by his antisocial or strange behavior?" True, he was suffering from being caught by the teacher and reported to the school principal, but was that the *center* of his suffering?

I was with the family only a few minutes when I realized the true meaning of his suffering was the fear that his parents' shaky marriage would break up. He had intuitively sensed that when he was stealing, his mother and father talked cooperatively with each other. When he was symptom-free, they resumed their squabbling. Being in trouble for stealing was a price he was willing to pay if it would keep his folks together. It was necessary to do marriage counseling in order for the boy's suffering—and symptoms—to be relieved.

A general guideline is that we usually need to look beyond the apparent source of the suffering. The systems approach does not *always* explain the motivation of children, but it is often useful in the diagnosis.

A second-grade girl was referred to me by a school psychologist for school phobia. Her mother often had to drag her to the car, drive to school, and then drag her into the classroom. The mother, stepfather, and children (aged seven to seventeen) all came for the counseling session. As we talked about where the hurting was for each family member at this time in their lives, two or three of the children mentioned the death of their biological father. A little later the real source of the girl's suffering became clear. She was not school phobic. She was afraid that her mother would die, just as her father had. Her father had died when she was not present. Therefore, she did not want to leave her mother alone. She wanted to "keep an eye" on her.

With this new information on the nature and cause of her suffering, it was possible to arrange a workable intervention plan with the aid of the school, including allowing her to call her home a few times a day until her fears decreased. This girl's situation illustrates the viewpoint that the more family members who are present for counseling, the greater the opportunity of accurately diagnosing the exact nature of the IC's suffering. It also suggests that as counselors we need to keep learning about family systems theory and practice so that we can make our interventions as meaningful as possible.[1]

Traditional psychotherapy has usually seen past family interactions as the cause of a child's symptoms. However, such psychotherapy has often overlooked the present family as resources in symptom reduction.

THE OVERWHELMING NATURE OF SUFFERING

Patricia Starck, a nurse educator, has done research on how patients perceive their suffering.[2] The patients, all hospitalized, had varying diagnoses of physical pathology. Yet on a "degree of suffering" scale, with 1 being minimum suffering and 10 being maximum suffering, the mean response was 6.4, which indicated a high degree of suffering. Starck noted that "this finding substantiates Frankl's view that suffering is like gas in a chamber; no matter how great or small, suffering tends to completely fill the human soul."[3]

Starck's research confirms the idea that as counselors we must attend to the pain of our clients. It is rather cold and ineffective to talk to clients about their "problem." It is more human, and more spiritual, to inquire about their suffering. *Any* suffering is felt so deeply by the client that the counselor must address it. It is useful to focus the diagnosis not just on the presenting problem, but on the *source of the pain,* as well.

WHEN THE SUFFERING CANNOT BE RELIEVED

A thirty-year-old woman came to talk about her deep suffering. She had trusted her husband implicitly during their ten years of marriage. But she had just discovered that he has had, at various times in the last five years, several different affairs. Her trust had, of course, blinded her to what were now obvious clues. We needed to work on many things, but the reduction of her suffering was not one of them. There was no way to relieve her pain.

When a client is experiencing great suffering, the best thing we as counselors can do is to let them express it. And, again, we help them localize the pain. When I asked her what her tears would say if they could talk, she said they were for her children more than for herself. The children deserved and needed an "in-house" dad. Later, when she has had time to grieve what is missing, she will be able to focus more on what is left.

She felt she had been gullible, and this was the cause of guilt and suffering for her. "Why didn't I see it earlier?" I began to use Socratic questioning in an attempt to help her find some meaning in her suffering. "Would you have preferred to have been suspicious of your husband all these years? That way you could have known of his unfaithfulness much sooner, and perhaps not have suffered so many years."

"Oh, no," she said. "I couldn't have lived that way." She believed that her trust of him was a good thing even though she was now in great pain. She began to feel less guilty when she realized that it was her trust which left her vulnerable. It also helped her to affirm that even if she had it to do over again, she would not have chosen suspicion as a way of married life. I think she left with greater self-respect, and she needed that. When she saw that it was the strength of her moral nature, rather than a weakness, that kept her from knowing the truth earlier, her prolonged suffering began to have some purpose.

Pain is a part of every life. We can, in a sense, hold ourselves upright and bear our pain bravely if we can find meaning in the suffering. But that is not true of misery which has a lack of purpose, or spiritlessness about it. Suppose that an adult has a phobia of syringes and needles. However, because of being exposed to a disease, he has to have a shot. With great fear he goes to the clinic and receives the shot. He has experienced anticipatory suffering, but the suffering has meaning because he can thus keep his health. But if a one-year-old is brought to the clinic to get a shot, he will likely be miserable because he cannot find any meaning in all this suffering, including the "betrayal" of his parents. If the hurting person can be helped to find the real meaning in the painful experience, he no longer is so miserable. It is by Socratic questioning that clients can often begin to discover the meaning.

FULFILLMENT IN SUFFERING

It is good that meaning can come through suffering because suffering is unavoidable. Some suffering is self-imposed because of sin. Other suffering is caused by sickness. But in addition, "there is a suffering beyond all sickness . . . the suffering which belongs to human life by the very nature and meaning of life."[4] One example of such existential suffering is the pain which is caused by change.

A couple and their three children—aged twenty-three, nineteen, and fourteen—came to me for counseling. The nineteen-year-old daughter is overcoming anorexia nervosa. I have counseled with her regularly for three months, and the family comes in together every now and then. The patient has been gaining weight slowly, averaging about a pound a week. Recently, she met her family at my office after seeing her physician and nutritionist, who monitored her progress and checked her weight. During our session she said to her family, "Oh, you'd probably like to know I gained three pounds this week." They clapped and one or two exclaimed, "Wow!" They could not have been more elated. Then I asked her what her feelings were about the weight gain. She cried and said, "I don't want to talk about it."

Her family was subdued and stunned by her reaction. I explained to them that change is painful. She would suffer in putting the weight back on just as she had suffered in taking the weight off. She was making a sacrifice in enduring the pain associated with change by requiring herself to eat when she did not want to. But the meaning of her suffering was that she was making steady progress toward renewed health. I think her family saw in a new way how hard she was working.

Suffering, of course, is also a part of Christian discipleship. As Braaten put it, "The glory of the Christian life in the world is hidden under the signs of suffering, humility, grief, disgrace, despair, and death."[5] Since suffering is a part of our human and spiritual legacy, we will not always be able to help clients reduce their pain. However, we can help them reduce needless misery, and we can comfort those who suffer.

CHAPTER NINETEEN

COUNSELING CHILDREN FOR MEANING

WHEN I WAS A CHILD, my family lived on a farm in Kansas. I will never forget the summer day when my father and I were out in the field cultivating corn. We took a break from the intense heat and back-breaking work to sit down under a shade tree and have a cool drink of water. We must have been talking about my future because I can remember Dad saying, "Paul, you have a good head on your shoulders. You're really going to amount to something." My father's affirmation and prediction had a big impact on me. It gave me confidence and hope, and it gave me meaning during my difficult early teen years. And because of that experience under the shade tree, I can more fully understand Bruno Bettelheim's views regarding children and meaning.

Bettelheim, a leading child psychiatrist, has said, "Today, as in times past, the most important and also the most difficult task in raising a child is helping him to find meaning in life."[1] Bettelheim goes on to say that to discover this meaning we must believe that we will make a "significant contribution to life—if not right now, then at some future time."[2] This was the meaning which my father helped this scared child discover, that I would make a "significant contribution to life."

Many children do not have even one adult with whom they can talk, or will talk, about things that matter. A great many "carefree kids" are actually in despair. Therefore, it is the privilege of the Christian counselor to listen to their concerns and to gently guide them in the process of discovering God's love and meaning for their lives.

THE PLACE OF THE FAMILY

Much of my counseling with children and youth is done in a family setting. That is where the resources are for change. I rarely see children by themselves, even though parents often want to send a ten-year-old to me to "straighten him out" (a painful metaphor—I usually visualize a steamroller bearing down on a child). I think many parents want to *send* rather than *take* their child to a counselor because they have given up and no longer see themselves as part of the change and growth process for their child.

A child's meaning is centered in his or her connection with the family. Historically, as counselors became aware of this, the old "child guidance" movement gradually changed into the current family counseling approach. To be of greatest use to children, pastors and other Christian counselors need to develop their *family* counseling skills as much as possible.

Meaning as a Resource in Family Counseling Sessions

A mother called wanting me to work with her eleven-year-old boy who was in trouble for bullying younger children in his elementary school. I asked her to come with her husband and both of their children. It is important, when possible, to have the other children in a family come as well as the one seen by the parents as needing help. This takes some of the pressure off the child in trouble, and provides additional resources for help. Operating as I do from the point of view that the parent-child bond is central to the child's meaning in life, I tried to figure out what was going on in this family.

Two things stood out by the end of the first session—the anger of the father and the shakiness of the marriage. After that first session, I worked several times with just the couple present. The husband had been suppressing his anger for years. He wanted to "tell off" his employer and his wife. Although he didn't want to leave either his job or his marriage, he sulked in both settings. He was able in the comparative safety of the counseling office to let his wife know what had been bothering him for a long time. She had some things to say to him as well. This cleared the air considerably at home, and made it a more pleasant place to be. He was sure that his employer would fire him if he said what he wanted to. So we did some role-playing in which I took the role of the employer, and then we reversed roles. This process took a little of the edge off his hostility because he began to understand his employer's point of view for the first time. Armed with the role-play experience and the newly felt support of his wife, he talked to his employer and was quite relieved that he did not feel enraged any more (and that he was not fired). After that encounter, his son's teacher reported that the bullying behavior had significantly decreased. I met with the total family one more time to help them look at their individual goals and their goals for the family, and how they each could be supportive of others in the future. We ended the counseling at that point.

What made the difference in the child's bullying? I believe he was misbehaving for two important reasons. As an eleven-year-old he was very concerned with the question, "How does a boy become a man?" I observed in the first counseling session that he looked at his father with a great deal of respect. He worked hard at imitating his dad. His dad wrote the script for anger and hostility every day, and his son, who was good at memorizing the lines, acted it out at school. When the father demonstrated courage and thereby reduced his hostility, his son could practice imitating more constructive behaviors.

The second factor in the boy's misbehavior was his anticipatory separation anxiety caused by his parent's angry relationship with each other. He feared their potential divorce. As Bettelheim has said, "There is no greater threat in life than that we will be deserted, left all alone . . . and the younger we are, the more excruciating is our anxiety when we feel deserted. . . . "[3] This threat-of-separation anxiety contributes to one child's withdrawal and another's acting out. When the marriage was seen by the children as stabilizing, the eleven-year-old began to stabilize, too.

So, the bullying behavior was successfully worked with by attending to the boy's two primary meanings in life—"How do I become a man?" and "Will my parents stay together, or will one or both desert me?" One of the exciting adventures of counseling is to seek out the meaning perspective of each client. This is a little like watching a three-ring circus when the "client" is a family. To the extent that the family does not contribute to the meaning of each individual member, the family experience becomes meaningless, or at least confusing to that member.

A life-long gift which can help our children lead meaningful lives is for us to provide them with an education in values. A fine resource for parents who are looking for help in this area is Paul Lewis's book, *Forty Ways to Teach Your Child Values.*[4] This book has chapters on "Decisions—How to Help Your Child Make Good Choices," "Chores, Children, and Character—They Go Together," "How Do We Teach Honesty?" and thirty-seven other topics. Paul Lewis is also the editor of *Dad's Only* newsletter, another valuable resource for parents.[5]

THE NEED TO REFRAME

Reframing is a technique used by many counselors to challenge and expand their clients' thinking. This technique can be used when we counsel with children, and when we counsel with adults who work with children. Selection Research, Inc. (SRI), developed a list, shown in a modified way in figure 5, of positive ways to interpret or reframe behaviors and qualities rather than relying on the negative judgments shown in the left column.[6] For example, some children need to be viewed not as tattletales but as justice-seekers, because they are motivated by a strong sense of justice. We thus correctly see the child as acting morally rather than immorally. This will enable us as counselors to be far more effective with the child.

New Ways to Talk about Children

Negative Comment or Label	Reframed Quality	Negative Comment or Label	Reframed Quality
tattletale	justice seeker	compulsive	efficient
stubborn	focused/committed/determined	silly	fun loving
fussy about food, clothing	discriminating	goofy	untamed creativity
too talkative	good relator	plain	natural
finicky eater	future gourmet/discriminating	shy	inner directed
doodles	creative	timid	careful
dawdles	easy going	dependent	connected
mouthy	expressive	fearful	careful risker
wants attention	speaks out needs	rigid	high sense of order

Figure 5

SRI has noted that we often make negative comments about children, or even other adults. We may complain that Bobby is very "hyper." But "what seems to be Bobby's 'problem' is often Bobby's strength. High energy level may someday carry him to completion on a complex task or be what fuels his championship swimming ability."[7]

Think of children you know who have been given a negative label. Then reframe that negative judgment into a positive quality. By affirming the child's goodness rather than focusing on the negative, you yourself will be able to realize the child's potential. In addition, the child will prosper because of the renewed approval of him or her.

The most important guideline in counseling children is to treat them with great respect. We should not treat them *as if* they are equals. They *are* equals. They have much to teach their counselors. As Pascal said, "Wisdom sends us to childhood."[8] Children work best with counselors who are not afraid of them, and are not condescending toward them. In fact, children have bailed me out many times when my family counseling boat was leaking. They are, fortunately, only too glad to help adults.

CHAPTER TWENTY

COUNSELING YOUTH FOR MEANING

RICHARD NELSON BOLLES has written an excellent book on meaning. In it he gives a diagram that offers direction to counselors who work with youth. Actually the concepts are true for persons of all ages.

The level at which people find themselves as they begin any new activity—kindergarten, junior high, college, a job, or marriage—is often one of confusion: *"What's happening?"* Youth need adults to let them know they are not abnormal or "weird" for feeling confused in a new situation. It goes with the territory.

As children or adolescents talk through their confusion with a caring adult, or as they work it through on their own (this usually takes longer and is more painful), they move into the level of *survival*. They know what's happening, or at least they think they do. Now they begin to work quietly, even desperately, to survive. One young woman talked about her year-old marriage using phrases like, "I'm being sucked in" (a whirlpool metaphor) to communicate her desperate fight for survival. The counselor can often provide a note of hope and love. These are the two components that keep the person going.

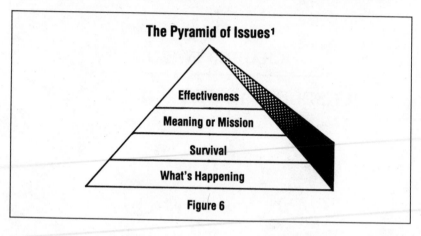

The Pyramid of Issues[1]

Effectiveness

Meaning or Mission

Survival

What's Happening

Figure 6

The third level is the turning point in any life situation, whether it be school, work, or retirement. We begin to sort out the *meaning* in life for our present situation. And we discover the *mission* that God has given us to perform.

The final, highest, level is to strive for as much *effectiveness* as we can in carrying out this mission. As you look at the four-level pyramid, you can see that the Christian counselor is in an excellent position to respond to children or adolescents as they transition from level to level.

Bolles's book is entitled *The Three Boxes of Life: And How to Get Out of Them*. The boxes are education, work, and retirement. We jump into the box of education when we are about five, then jump out of it and into the box of work around the age of eighteen or twenty. Finally, we crawl out of the box of work in our mid-sixties and into the box of retirement. Bolles suggests that we get out of the boxes by thinking of a "pie" graph with three pieces—learning, working, and playing.[2]

That way we can include more of one or the other at any time in our lives.

If we are going to be useful in helping others stay out, or get out, of the boxes, we will need to take a fresh look at ourselves from time to time in this regard. My father used to tell me that we could never save up play for the future. We either played as we went through life or we lived a life without playing. It is a saying that I need to remind myself of from time to time. Most youth still feel the need to play. Many parents and counselors do not, and therefore have difficulty connecting with the younger generation.

But youth want to do more than play. "Youth was made for heroism and not for pleasure," according to Ernest Becker.[3] That statement has the ring of truth. And it supports the significance of the question for discovering meaning: "What is life asking of me?" This is not a question to which pleasure seekers know how to respond. It is a question for heroes and for all who have a vision that extends beyond themselves to the world in which they live.

I once heard a church speaker say, "Now one thing you young people need to know is . . . ." I watched them roll their eyes and slump as if to say, "Oh, no, not again!" Youth have been told a great many things and most are tired of being told. But they usually respond positively when they are challenged and questioned. Therefore, youth counselors would do well to gain skill in Socratic questioning.

In a Viktor E. Frankl Merit Award Contest, high school students were given the opportunity to write essays on meaning.[4] Many quoted a variety of statements from Frankl that in some way spoke for them. The statement most often quoted came from *Man's Search for Meaning* and centered on the need to search not for abstract meanings in life, but rather for a specific meaning in life: " . . . everyone must carry out a concrete assignment that demands fulfillment. Therein he cannot be replaced, nor can his life be repeated."[5]

The high frequency of selection of this particular passage indicates that this is one thing adults cannot tell youth. We cannot dictate to young people their mission in life. We can share the gospel of Jesus Christ with them, or lead a small group Bible study. However, each person needs to discover his or her own mission because it is concrete and unique, given by God only to that one person. This concept underlines Bolles's idea that once we have determined "What's happening," and how to survive, we need to search out our meaning and mission in life, and find how to be effective in performing it. This is where the heroism, the great effort, comes in. Some adolescents who are still in a stage of confusion may be unwilling to struggle with meaning. It is therefore important to use the power of the counselor-client relationship at this point to keep the client working, because it is the discovery of meaning that will eliminate the confusion.

Last week I talked with a nineteen-year-old client who is beginning to overcome an eating disorder. She said she and her boyfriend wanted to get married, and she asked if I thought she was ready. I said no. When she asked why, I replied, "If you crawl from one nest to another, you will never learn to fly." She was upset with me, of course. I told her that I thought I knew what she wanted from life, but I wasn't sure what she thought life expected from her. It took a while to communicate the question, but later she said that she really wanted to be a good mother, to give her children a good experience growing up. I could see then, given her perceived mission in life, why she wanted to get married right away. Next time I plan to talk with and question her about prior experiences she needs in order to be the best mother possible.

I have asked many college sophomores to respond to the question, "What is my purpose in life?" These nineteen- and twenty-year-olds gave a wide range of answers, including the following representative samples:

"I guess maybe my purpose is to be a servant."

"I believe my purpose in life is to continually strive to be a better person."

"My purpose in life is to make something of myself and be proud of what I'm doing."

"I feel that God has given me the gift of artistic ability, and the desire to share it with others."

"My purpose in life is to be the best me I can be. This means developing and using my God-given talents in the way that will do the most good."

"I believe that my purpose in life is to learn what it means to love God and others as well as I love myself."

"I don't believe that our life must have a purpose here on earth."

"I know my purpose in life is to help people. But sometimes it's hard to know how to do it."

The overwhelming majority of the responses were altruistic in nature. Many were also spiritual. I am not suggesting that these responses are representative of all youth. But they provide evidence to support the point of view that in counseling youth we need to build on their motivation to help others and, in many cases, to serve God.

As adults we often seek "homeostasis," stability in our lives. But youth are seeking to avoid boredom and to find adventure. Therefore, challenge is an important part of the repertoire of the youth counselor. It is the heroic quest itself that has meaning. As counselors we need to challenge youth to move beyond the survival level and find the courage to carry out their unique mission in life. Through Socratic dialogue we can help them discover that mission and the necessary resources and strategies to begin it.

CHAPTER TWENTY-ONE

MEANING AS A RESOURCE IN MARRIAGE COUNSELING

ELIE WIESEL WROTE that "God made man because he loves stories."[1] Looked back upon, marriages are stories full of love, loneliness, reconciliation, trauma, anger, and joy. Each marriage has its beginning and its ending. I believe that a primary *meaning* of marriage, and one that is often overlooked by marriage counselors, is the *story* of the marriage. Even if the marriage is only six months old the story has begun. And if the couple has been married thirty-five years and is considering divorce, they need to review their long story carefully before ending that story by their own action.

GETTING THEIR STORY

The counselor needs to obtain a family history (the antecedents of the marriage story) from each of the spouses, and then the story of their own marriage. This process serves as a reminder to each spouse that there is more to their marriage than the present crisis. Usually people who come for marriage counseling have dysfunctional memories. Their heads are so befogged by hurt, anger, and often hate and revenge, that their memories are blocked. The problem is that they think their memories are intact. But listen to them recollect a common incident. They relate two widely differing stories, not a common story, because of the working of time and individual mental rehearsals. Also couples "rewrite their history" as they experience a new conflict. The counselor who can help clients distance from some of their symptoms of hurt and anger can begin to draw out the real story of their marriage.

When a couple comes with an urgent crisis, then the crisis must be dealt with as the first item of business. However, as soon as possible I begin to get their story. I call it "Getting your story," rather than "Taking your family history." I use the genogram as the basic tool for showing the story.

The Modified Genogram

The genogram developed by Murray Bowen and others is a tool I use in nearly all my counseling—individual, marriage, and family—because of its ability to graphically portray the story of the person, couple, or family. It is simply a chart borrowed (and modified) from the field of genealogy. Murray Bowen has been a pioneer in developing the genogram to portray graphically the impact of one generation on successive generations. He describes in detail his "multigenerational transmission" theory in his *Family Therapy in Clinical Practice.*[2] His theory is research-based, a careful study of the history of many families. Bowen would often trace back a hundred years or more to see if there was a tendency to transmit family characteristics, including illnesses. He concluded that there was a multigenerational transmission of basic family patterns.[3] Such patterns become quite graphic when the counselor uses a genogram to visualize the family story.

Different counselors have their own method of using abbreviations and symbols. Most use a square to represent men and a circle for women. However, one family therapist, a woman, uses circles for both men and women because "men are square enough as it is!" I include siblings, parents, and often grandparents of the couple, as well as any children and grandchildren.[4] Again, the particular aspect of genograms that I want to demonstrate is their value in recreating meaning in the marriage by reconstructing the story. A very simple genogram is shown in figure 7.

This hypothetical three-generational genogram centers on Ed and Peg. Let's suppose they came for marriage counseling. This genogram, if true, would be much more complete, showing such important items as illnesses, miscarriages, educational achievements, church affiliation, and dates of all significant happenings, including births, severe illnesses, and deaths. If there were several family traumas around the birth of Peg, for example, these become an important part of her story and of the marriage story. If Ed were converted when their son John was fourteen and became more loving, that also becomes a part of the stories.

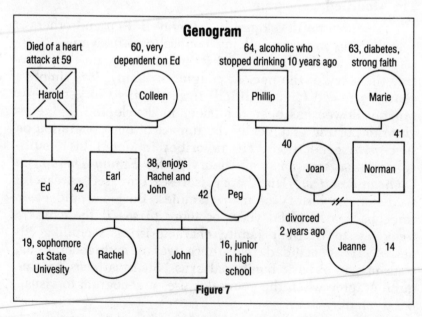

Figure 7

We can see some intergenerational connections that may be causing difficulty in the marriage. The dependency of his mother on Ed may place a strain on the marriage. Also Peg grew up the child of an alcoholic and may have come into the marriage with a large emotional debt. On the positive side, Earl is a caring uncle for Ed and Peg's children, and Peg's mother has a strong faith. The contribution of a genogram is that it provides a graphic presentation of the story of the couple.

One young couple came for counseling because the husband was beginning to talk about divorce. The presenting problem was that of the wife's dislike of sex. Their sexual relationship had been generally unsatisfactory throughout their two-year marriage. A metaphor for this was that she would hug him warmly as he left for work. She knew he did not have time for sex then. However, when he came home from work and tried to hug her, she crossed her arms in front of her body with her palms on her shoulders to distance herself from him and an embrace that might lead to sex.

I asked them to put sex on hold for three weeks while we met weekly to look at their shared life and its meaning. The moratorium on sex wasn't a problem; it just made it official. I discovered their individual stories and their joint story by constructing a genogram. We talked about many positive things. Why did they choose each other? What about their spiritual kinship? What activities did they do together before they became resentful of each other? What were their individual goals and dreams and their couple goals and dreams? This process, of course, was one of dereflection. They had both been hyper-reflected on sex, a highly significant component of their marriage, but not the *only* component. It was important to focus for awhile on the other parts of their story which had great meaning. They laughed some when they talked of the walks they used to take together. They had a way of talking about little things they saw along the way. The laughter also helped the dereflection process. It should be noted that although they both felt somewhat rejected and resentful, they were not full of bitterness. Their anger had not yet gotten cold.

Treatment consisted of a referral to a gynecologist, a number of individual counseling sessions concerning the wife's differentiation from her mother who "still sees sex as dirty," and the couple's use of the "sexual pleasuring" technique. I loaned them books during this time, including Charlie and Martha Shedd's *Celebration in the Bedroom*, a joyful, "impious" approach to married sex.[5] We ended counseling after they reported satisfaction with their sexual relationship, and after we had talked together about the new meaning of their marriage. They sent a card a year later to announce the birth of their first child, and called me about a year after that to get the name of a counselor in another city for friends of theirs (and to update me on their continuing story).

I think that taking time to help this couple discover the strengths and the meaning of their story together not only dereflected and relaxed them, but it helped them see that their marriage was worth saving. The center of the meaning was their account of their own spiritual journeys before they met, their times of prayer together before they were married, and the beginning of their marriage with a genuine commitment to each other in the presence of Christ.

Meeting with the Family of Origin

Sometimes when I am doing marriage counseling and we get to the "bottom line," it sounds like this: "If worse comes to worst, I will choose my parents instead of you." This is an anguished admission of a truth from one spouse that both have known for a long time. At this point I ask the dependent adult to bring his or her parents and siblings (the total family of origin, if possible) for one or more counseling sessions. The spouse is nearly always terrified when I make this request. But about half of these clients, with great courage, make the invitation. Those geographically available from the family of origin usually come, some traveling hundreds of miles. So I have had many sessions with adult children in their twenties and thirties (once in a while in the early forties) and parents in their fifties, sixties, and seventies. Usually all the siblings are enmeshed (bound together by guilt) with the parents.

The family members say things that have needed to be said for a long time. I have never had one of these sessions that has

142

not been frightening for all of us, nor without benefit to the family. The parents, of course, want autonomous children, but don't want to let go of them. I can tell when the process is working for the spouse with whom I am especially concerned. This person goes through a brief, terror-filled time of feeling like an abandoned child as the differentiation process is reopened and continued. When there has been some healing, there are new possibilities in the marriage because the individual has finally "left home." Dependent behavior is both a symptom and a cause of meaninglessness, and gives direction to the counselor for treatment—differentiation. If the family of origin is unavailable, the counselor may still help the client get "unstuck" through individual counseling.

THE PASSAGE OF TIME—EPISODES OR JOURNEY?

The rationale for the above view of marriage as a story has to do with the way we view time. Does our life consist of a series of episodes, or is it all connected—a journey? This question is of great significance to the quest for meaning. If life is simply episodical, then meaning is greatly reduced because there can be no sense of perspective, of story, of connectedness. If life is a journey, then each of the episodes can have meaning, including the opening and closing episodes—birth and death.

The Episodical Nature of Life

As we look at life around us, the evidences at first seem compelling for viewing life as a series of unconnected events. Most schools, including church schools, are finely graded with pre-school classes, kindergarten, first grade, and so on. Human development books discuss ages and stages. Television serials, whether soap operas or sitcoms, are episodical. Even our church worship services can be viewed in a disconnected way from one week to the next. Many people reduce life to three primary episodes: Education, work, and retirement.[6]

Life (and Marriage) as a Journey

One of the major evidences that life is connected is that God holds us responsible for our actions. Our past, present, and future are of one piece in terms of responsibility. Contrast that with the legal view of insanity. If someone commits murder and is later judged to have been insane at the time, the defendant may be pronounced "not guilty by reason of insanity." However, in that plea of insanity that person loses not only the legal obligations that go with responsibility, but he also loses part of the essence of what it means to be human—that is, responsibility for one's acts.

We need to be responsible in the journey of marriage, but we cannot, individually, control that journey. The truth is, we cannot control any journey. We set out on a vacation and plan to follow a schedule. However, if the car breaks down, we lose control of our time (and money) very rapidly. We plan a business trip using commercial flights. But if a flight is cancelled because of weather or mechanical problems, or if the suitcase containing materials for a seminar presentation is lost, we again lose control of the trip. In this respect, marriage is like all other journeys. John Steinbeck made that clear in discussing the nature of journeys in his book, *Travels with Charlie.*[7] Charlie was a poodle who accompanied Steinbeck in a pick-up camper on a meandering, friendly investigation of the United States. Steinbeck noted:

> We find after years of struggle that we do not take a trip; a trip takes us. . . . In this a journey is like marriage. The certain way to be wrong is to think you control it. I feel better now, having said this, although only those who have experienced it will understand it.[8]

The Bible is careful to make clear that life is a journey. There is even connectedness between earth and heaven. Resurrection has to do with continuity as well as change. And the Bible is clear that *marriage* should also be a unified story: "That is why a man leaves his father and mother and is united with his wife, and they become one" (Gen. 2:24). A helpful tool which provides a sense of story and meaning to counseling with couples is Bill Coleman's *It's Been a Good Year: The Anniversary Book.*[9] It is an upbeat resource that provides spouses with new ideas for surviving struggles and celebrating togetherness.

CHAPTER TWENTY-TWO

FINDING MEANING IN THE WORKPLACE

ONE OF THE MOST difficult things I do as a counselor is to try to help people whose work has become drudgery. It's like trying to get a fire going with wood that has wet snow all over it. However, the reality is that sometimes the meaning does wane in one's job—or even one's career. It is useful to help clients discover whether the meaninglessness is a part of their work or a part of them. We do this by finding the clients' mission in life (what God, or life, is asking of them). Then we help them look carefully at their job to see if it can provide this meaning.

When clients want to talk about recareering, I recommend Richard Nelson Bolles's book, mentioned earlier, *The Three Boxes of Life: And How to Get Out of Them.* If it is someone

145

fairly new in the workforce, I recommend his annually updated job book, *What Color Is Your Parachute?*[1] Both these
books are done with great skill and humor. This helps readers
to relax. Bolles operates from the concept of meaning. He has
the readers work through exercises and experiences until they
begin to discover what sort of work would appeal to their interests, utilize their skills, *and* help them carry out their mission
in life. Bolles says regarding work and mission that we need to
find a deep answer to the issue: "That is to find, beyond meaning, some ultimate goal or mission for your life, that drives you
on with a kind of sacrificial, burning passion."[2]

When we are counseling with clients whose work is no longer
attractive to them, we can use such Socratic questions as:
"What *parts* of your current job excite you?" "What aspects of
your work can you 'take or leave'?" "What activities do you do
each day in your job which are totally devoid of meaning for
you?" "You know what it is that you don't want in a job. What
do you want?" "Describe the ideal job. If you could 'paint' the
ideal job and walk into the painting, what would it look like?"
"Please describe your mission in life, what God requires of
you. What does life expect of you? How will you pay your rent
for living on this earth? What will you give back to life?" "How
well does your present job fit your mission?" (Remember that
in a real world most jobs and missions don't match 100 percent!) "How well does your ideal job fit your mission?" It takes
a while, but clients usually begin to discover the source of
meaninglessness. Let's suppose the lack of meaning is *inside*
the person.

WHEN THE EMPTINESS IS IN THE WORKER

There have been a number of times in the last 15 years when
I found myself just "chasing the wind" in my work and knowing that the fascination was gone. During three of those low
points I sought and was offered other jobs. But I realized each
time that the emptiness was inside me, and I would be taking
it along with me to another state. So I talked with my wife and
two or three other close friends, and the joy at work gradually
came back. I learned through this informal counseling that
there had been several factors involved, such as tiredness

caused by pushing myself too hard. However, the biggest factor in my situation all three times was a crisis in my confidence. I felt I was not doing as good a job teaching and counseling as I knew how to do. Actually, I learned I had been judging my performance a bit too harshly. Even so, I did seek help to improve in these areas.

If the emptiness is inside, the counselor can follow some of the many guidelines given throughout this book for helping the client with personal meaning. In addition, it is useful to examine the client's job. Can more meaning be "squeezed" from the job? Can the worker attend to relationships as well as tasks at work by making life better for fellow employees or, if it is a service occupation, for those served? Could the job take on more meaning if it is viewed as a necessary step to a more meaningful job?

A high-achieving competent executive was passed over when it was time for promotions. He lost job satisfaction and self-confidence. He came to see me as a friend for a counseling session. Several months later he talked with me about his crisis, our session together, and the direction he took to rediscover meaning in his work:

> I felt like I had failed, so I got into a depressed state. At the deepest part of that is when I decided to come see you. I can't tell you what either of us said—the exact statements. I know there were some statements that were supportive and some questions that made me think about things. When I walked out of there and went home I felt good. . . . And my wife was very helpful to me. She kept me going. She is a well-grounded Christian and she gave me a lot of spiritual support. I remember you told me, "It could get worse." I don't think it ever did get worse, but it didn't get better overnight, either. I'd feel good, and then a day or two later I'd get back down again. A couple of people at work gave me some ideas about improving my job performance and I started taking some action and doing something about it. Things have turned out well. I had two or three other jobs I could have taken, but I'm glad I stayed with this one.

I can't remember my responses to him, either. I do know that I pointed out his very significant strengths, which he was not able to see at the moment. Then I asked some Socratic questions about his work and his Christian mission. Despite his crisis in confidence he still believed that his work was a valid way of carrying out that mission. With the support of his wife and colleagues, and with his own determination, he was able to regain his confidence and his job satisfaction.

WHEN THE EMPTINESS IS IN THE WORK

I was waiting for a taxi in front of the airport to take me to a nursing home, where I was going to lead some workshops. A van stopped in front of me, and the driver motioned for me to get in. He worked for a cab company, and it was his job to transport residents and guests to and from nursing homes and homes for the handicapped. The van was specially outfitted with a lift. On the way to the nursing home we talked.

He was about fifty, and he had been an accountant most of his professional life. The last five years of that work had been as vice-president and comptroller of a large firm in the city. But several years ago his work began to lose meaning. He used to love helping his company make money and spend it wisely. He stayed with it a year or two after his interest in the work declined, but his heart just wasn't in it. He wanted out of finance. It didn't mean anything to him anymore. Now for the last few years he had been driving this van. He knew most of the kids and many of the nursing home residents by name. He obviously *loved* his job. It was fun to watch the way he connected with each of his riders. This was not just a job. It was a calling. I don't know whether he had counseling on recareering, or if he just picked up the "Help Wanted" ads one day. We didn't have time to talk about that. But whatever he did, it worked.

Networking is an important area for counselors to utilize in making this process work. An engineer wanted out. His work was no longer appealing. So through my professional network, I was able to refer him to a job placement office which specialized in executive recareering help. This involved a careful self-study of his marketable job skills and culminated in the creation of an accurate resumé. While he was getting help there, I worked with him on the subject of meaning in life, and raised such questions as what he thought life was asking of him. We discovered that he had good teaching skills and he liked working with people. He therefore decided to recareer into consulting work.

Recareering usually requires tremendous courage. When talking with a client about the risk involved, it is useful to discuss the pros and cons of change. There are definite, very apparent risks involved in changing careers, such as the possible loss of retirement benefits. These possibilities need to be carefully weighed. There are also dangers, less apparent, in not changing, such as the potential damage to one's physical and mental health of continuing for years and years doing work that is boring. These risks also need to be carefully examined.

PERIODIC INNER RENEWAL

We need frequent renewals in our lives, our relationships (including our relationship with God), and our work. If we undergo constant *internal* renewal, we can keep the quality of our lives, and continue our relationships (not feel the need to change spouses or friends). We can develop rather than lose our faith, and maintain our present careers (if they have sufficient meaning). If we do not have these internal renewals, we will seek external renewals. These may include wanting to move, to change jobs, or to seek new relationships.

CHAPTER TWENTY-THREE

COUNSELING THE RETIRED AND ELDERLY FOR MEANING

ONE SUMMER MANY YEARS AGO, I took a trip to tell each of my three brothers and my sister that I loved them. Bill, our youngest son, who had just graduated from high school, went with me. We were in the car a total of sixty-five hours. When it was my turn to drive, he read aloud to me from John Steinbeck's *Travels with Charlie*.[1] I began to realize the verity of Steinbeck's statement, "We do not take a trip; a trip takes us." It was happening at the moment. Then came another amazing line as we were on the last leg of the trip from Detroit back to Nebraska. Steinbeck and Charlie had seen all they wanted and were on their way home. However, they still had hundreds of miles to travel to reach their home.

Steinbeck said, "Who has not known a journey to be over and dead before the traveler returns?"[2] He went on to say that his own journey had started "long before I left, and was over before I returned."[3] From that point on, the hills became obstructions rather than friends. And for those last several hundred miles, "All the food along the way tasted like soup, even the soup."[4]

Bill and I both reflected on that thought because we had just crossed the Mississippi River from Illinois into Iowa. We just wanted to be plopped in our living-room chairs, but we still had the rest of the trip to make.

It occurred to me at that moment that this same idea was a metaphor for many retired and elderly people: The journey is over, but the trip isn't. One of the questions I am asked most frequently by nursing home staff members is, "How do I answer a resident who says to me nearly every day, "I just want to die; why can't I die?" I like what Lawrence LeShan says, "We don't have to give the answers; we just have to hear the questions."[5] Only God knows the answer to that question. But even though we can't give an *answer*, we can give a *response*. For instance, I have heard some nurses say, "I don't know. But I love you, and I'm glad you're alive and here!"

I've had the opportunity to work for seven summers training staff members and residents in helping/caring/counseling skills in seven different retirement center/nursing homes.[6] These homes represent nearly every major geographical section of the country. I made six to eight visits to most of the homes and conducted small group seminars each visit, with a total of 450 staff members and 114 residents. The retirement center residents ranged in age from approximately 75 to 96. There were some groups whose average age was about 90. These residents taught me a great deal about growing old and continuing to live a life filled with meaning.

I developed a curriculum for the training that aimed at deepening meaning in life for both staff and residents by the use of a relational approach.[7] We did this in several ways. One was by the use of the "two-list" approach. Staff members work hard and fast in a retirement center/nursing home setting. Most make out a mental or literal list of things to do each day.

I talked with them about making out a second list, one which had the names of two or three residents or staff members with whom they would like to deepen a relationship. We need to attend to *relationships* as well as to *tasks* each day, or meaning declines.

Another method used to increase meaning was the application of the discovery approach. The staff was challenged to "discover" a resident each day. Discovery was used in the sense that Carolyn B. Stevens used it in her book, *Special Needs of Long-Term Patients.* She noted that some residents have to lie in bed just waiting for the aides. "Physical care is only one half of what is needed. To give the other half, you have to look inside them. Someone is in there."[8] That is discovery! However, it is very difficult to discover some elderly persons because of sensory impairments. It is difficult to discover others because of barriers common to all ages, such as shyness, grief, and anger.

Another emphasis in the training was to alert the staff to receive from residents. As we age, we typically have fewer opportunities to give, and more to receive. If this is carried to an extreme it can be devastating to a purpose for living. It is all receiving and no giving. We no longer are needed. Since it is more blessed to give than to receive, we need to make sure that the aging have that blessing. One of the greatest gifts we can give to someone is to receive from them—a flower, a word of advice, or a smile.

One aspect of receiving was to learn from the residents. The elderly have a great deal to teach us if we listen. Sometimes we can learn to chuckle about life. Bruce Bliven shared just such a learning:

What have I learned in eighty-three years? I have learned, if you get mugged in the street, don't yell help, yell fire. Nobody wants to come to a mugging, but everyone is interested in a fire.[9]

REGAINING MEANING

In one home in the midwest a number of residents and staff members said I should go see Mrs. M because she had an unusual story to tell. This retirement center/nursing home had five levels of care—from fully independent living to skilled nursing care (as in a hospital). Most residents entered one of the lower levels of care and eventually needed skilled nursing. Mrs. M had entered the skilled nursing unit and worked her way the other direction until she was now in a fully independent living area. One summer morning, I had the opportunity to visit her. She poured coffee for us and began to tell her story.

She had been a pastor's wife most of her life. Her husband died soon after retiring from the pastorate. She grieved, of course, but something else happened. She became, in her own words, a "whiner." She complained, whined, isolated herself, sat a lot—and became ill. Her joints didn't work right, her energy was low, and her "heart was weak." She was finally admitted to the skilled nursing unit of this home, where she kept asking the question, "Why me, Lord?"

She had to be dressed each morning. Finally, one day a nurse's aide, who was tough as nails and just as sharp, put her dress four or five feet away from her. Mrs. M whined, "But I can't dress myself!" The nurse's aide responded, "Well, there are men who will be going up and down that hall. Do you want to be decent or not?" Now one of Mrs. M's main purposes in life was to be decent, so she finally got her dress on. Later the nurse's aide came back, and Mrs. M said "You know I can't button it." The nurse's aide said, "You'll find a way," and left again. The aide's actions may appear to have been unkind. But I had a chance to observe her because she was in a number of the seminars, and I often saw her working with patients. As a matter of fact, she treated residents kindly and had a gentle touch. She also believed she should not do something for them that they could do themselves.

From that point on, Mrs. M began to become more responsible. Apparently this intervention by the nurse's aide was also a time when Mrs. M was thinking beyond just herself. She said she began to get better when she stopped asking the question, "Why me, Lord?" and started asking, "What do you want me to do, Lord?" Armed only with a new question and a nurse's aide's belief in her, she had worked her way, with great effort, to the apartment in which we were drinking coffee. She was now working as a volunteer in the nursing home. She attended Bible studies, and her life had renewed purpose.

CHECKING ON THE MEANING OF A CHOICE

I was leading a retirement seminar at a church when a woman in the group said, "Would you talk to my husband about retiring from the farm and moving to town?" He was right beside her, so we talked. They were about seventy years old. She desperately wanted to leave the farm and move to the city. But he obviously loved farming. I asked him what farming meant to him, supposing that he would talk about being outside, or putting his hands in the warm soil, or controlling his own time, or freedom. But he most enjoyed the *challenge* of farming. The same things that were driving others off the farm—drouths, embargos, high interest, and low prices for products—were adventures for him. He loved the uncertainty and the resulting need to respond to a new challenge.

I could see that he needed challenges to have a life full of meaning. Had he thought of other challenges beside farming? We talked about the need to transition to new challenges as he got older that would not require so much physical activity, such as consulting with other farmers. I could see why his wife wanted help with him. I only hope that a seed was planted. My method of intervention involved the use of a Socratic question, "What does farming mean to you?" If we do not ask such a question, we tend to respond to our *own* meaning rather than the client's meaning.

Gail Sheehy's book, *Pathfinders*, is the account of her study of well people.[10] Her three-year research program involved the completion of sixty thousand Life History Questionnaires. She distilled from the data "The Ten Hallmarks of Well-Being." Number one on the list was "My life has meaning and direction."[11] She noted that:

This is the characteristic that correlated most closely with optimum life satisfaction. People of high well-being find meaning in an involvement with something beyond themselves: a work, an idea, other people, a social objective.[12]

The retired no longer have the meaning that comes from doing their job well. On the other hand, their new-found control over their time gives them a whole new freedom to be "response-able." Some may recareer, others will serve as volunteers in the human services, while still others will discover creative abilities they never knew they had. By the use of Socratic questions we can help our older clients to look "beyond themselves," as Sheehy has suggested.

What about those who don't want to do *anything*? Well, maybe they need to rest for a year or two. However, I think that often "I don't want to do anything" means "I have nothing to offer." At this point the counselor can help the client do a strengths inventory and then challenge the client with the question, "Who else will finish those tasks that only you are able to do?"

CHAPTER TWENTY-FOUR

SELF-ESTEEM AND MEANING

SHE WAS AT MID-LIFE and was engaged in a life and death struggle with meaninglessness. She described that struggle and its relationship to her lack of self-esteem in an honest, graphic manner:

I need to determine if I possess any value in order to decide if there is any hope or meaning to my existence. With no value there is no hope or meaning. For the past two years I have been aimlessly wandering from colleges, college majors, jobs, and residences. I have been desperately trying to maintain the image of being strong and in control. In reality I am weak, totally out of control, and scared to death. I seem to be searching for something. Maybe I am really searching for me. God only knows I have no concept of who "me" is. In order to find me, I need to determine just who me is and if there is any importance to my existence. I cannot do this by going every route possible, but only by following the direct and most painful one. I have to stop taking detours, dead ends, and constantly fighting. This has been too costly. I am not even sure if there is much of me left to find.

Does it work to "search for me"? Self-discovery and even self-actualization may be overrated unless the end is to serve God and others. The push for self-actualization in the 1960s turned into narcissism in the 1970s and emptiness in the 1980s. This sequence seems logical in looking back. As we pursued self-actualization by seeking a life goal that focused on self, it was natural that the "me decade" would emerge. The next step in the sequence, after spending a great deal of time focusing on self, was the painful realization that seeking self-fulfillment and happiness were counter-productive goals without significant meaning.

But a problem remains. The evidences are irrefutable that turning our attention inward toward self-fulfillment actually results in self-emptying. Yet we still want self-fulfillment, and it seems to me a natural desire of loving ourselves.

A new client of mine had a goal—to feel better about herself, to overcome a lack of self-esteem. She is a mother of two who works full-time in the home. She attributes her lack of self-esteem to an intergenerational legacy—her mother and grandmother both have a sense of low self-worth. Should I have said to her, "You should not seek personal fulfillment; you should not seek to feel better about yourself"? I don't think so. She has been buffeted enough by circumstances without having a counselor give this kind of advice.

SELF-ESTEEM AND PRIDE

Both self-esteem and pride (used in the biblical, negative sense) involve a high estimate of ourselves. But pride is sinful because it involves comparison with others whom God has also created—"I am better than . . . " or "I am worse than . . . ." Both comparisons are wrong. "To be humble is not to make comparisons," said Dag Hammarskjöld.[1]

Both self-esteem and pride are a part of the spiritual dimension of life; they are not just *psychological* characteristics. Because of this belief, and because the client above was a committed Christian, I responded to her in the following vein: I asked if she regularly put others down. She replied that she very seldom did this, in fact, she saw this practice as being wrong. Then I inquired whether she put herself down. Yes, she did this regularly. She criticized herself and frequently judged herself as not being worth much. The next step was to pose a moral question: If it was wrong to judge and put down others whom God had created, was it then right to put herself down, who also was created by God? This was a new way to view her situation. She had been able to feel sorry for herself and to feel spiritual at the same time. Now if she adopted this new point of view that was compelling to her, she would need to second God's motion that she was worth as much as anyone else, or rule him out of order.

Morton Kelsey has put it strongly, "It is just as morally wrong to dislike, despise, and devalue ourselves as it is to have these attitudes toward others."[2] In one Peanuts series, Charlie Brown was feeling very discouraged. Lucy gave him a whack, and said that sometimes a little physical pain relieves emotional pain. I think it is also true that a little *moral* pain can relieve emotional pain. My client is now face to face with the moral pain of contradicting God's evaluation of her. If she, because of this, stops doing negative self-talk, she will begin feeling better about herself. I should note that she is a fine person, an excellent family member, and one who is known for reaching out in Christian compassion to others. If she had been clearly violating other moral laws, I would have responded to her differently than I did.

Perhaps the most difficult kinds of clients for me to work with are ones who see themselves as having gone through much suffering because they are the *special* targets of God's judgment. Usually, the situation has been that they have brought much of the pain on themselves by impulsiveness, anger, or a lack of hard work. Rollo May has said that *"condemning ourselves is the quickest way to get a substitute sense of worth. . . .* The self-condemning person is very often trying to show how important he is that God is so concerned with punishing him."[3] This person needs to be confronted gently and directly with the pride involved in this maneuver.

LIVING BEYOND OURSELVES

Once we agree with God that we are worthwhile, we can do those things in life that will be genuinely self-fulfilling and full of meaning. Frankl said that there are three ways to discover meaning in life: "1) by doing a deed; 2) by experiencing a value; and 3) by suffering."[4] The first has to do with accomplishing a task. The second way is by experiencing nature—such as a sense of wonder while viewing the Grand Canyon—or experiencing a person—like loving or being loved. The third way of discovering meaning is to find the true meaning of our suffering. A thirty-year-old woman was almost over her binging-purging cycle that had lasted five years. She had decreased her vomiting of food from fifteen or twenty times a week to two or three times a month. Despite her hard-won progress, she was reluctant to put her bulimia entirely behind her. I realized that before she could let go of it, she needed to assign a meaning to her suffering for those years. And we could not manufacture a meaning. It had to be discovered. As we talked about what is different now that she has been through so much pain, she found that she was providing more nutritious meals for her family than she formerly had. As the result of working with a nutritionist, she had gotten rid of sugary, fatty foods, and replaced them with simple, healthful foods. That she would be able to affect positively the life-long health of her children because of her own suffering had great meaning to her. This helped her feel good about herself and her progress. She was now living beyond herself.

Weakness

When people say they are weak, I think it is often useful to agree with that estimate. *Of course* they don't feel they have the strength to cope with life. That low estimate of one's

159

strength is, at least sometimes, a part of the human condition. I like to mention J. R. R. Tolkien's *The Hobbit* and his *Lord of the Rings* series.[5] Bilbo and Frodo were chosen, through no effort of their own, to go on an epic quest to save their world from destruction. They were hobbits, weak little creatures whose only claim to fame was that they just loved to eat—hardly hero material! Yet Tolkien's use of hobbits was not accidental. Tolkien's point of view concerning weakness is discussed in a letter which is part of an amazing collection, *The Letters of J. R. R. Tolkien.*[6] The book is worth reading because it reveals so much about Tolkien's Christian life and experience. Discussing his use of hobbits as heroes, he says that "the great policies of world history, 'the wheels of the world,' are often turned not by the Lords and Governors, even gods, but by the seemingly unknown and weak. . . ."[7]

Celebrating our weakness, or at least accepting it, is of course a biblical concept, "For when I am weak, then I am strong" (2 Cor. 12:10 NIV). It is the Lord who brings strength out of weakness by giving us courage.

THE PLACE OF COURAGE—AND ENCOURAGEMENT

I have become convinced that we could prevent a great deal of meaninglessness with our family, friends, colleagues at work, fellow church members, and others if we would do two things: 1) make "brave statements," and 2) encourage. These interventions heighten self-esteem.

Brave Statements

The first person I heard use the phrase "brave statements" was Sid Simon in his values clarification workshops. Here are some examples of such statements which I have used with clients:

"If you keep on living for the next five years like you're living now, what will happen to you?" (I've had people respond to this with, "I'd probably be dead!")

"Are you aware that you are blowing away students with your anger?" (to an otherwise fine college instructor—who was not aware of this).

"I wouldn't say what I'm going to say to you if I didn't care about our relationship" (to a fellow committee member whom I thought was monopolizing committee time).

"Where does God fit into your plans and goals?" (to a friend).

"The affair you're contemplating will bring more suffering than you can imagine to you, your lover, your husband, your children, and your parents" (to a client).

These all took some courage because I cared about each person and could not confront them in a detached way.

While I can give a few examples of "brave statements," there are many more times that I have taken the coward's way out and said nothing. I couldn't find the courage, or didn't care enough. It is too bad, because such statements could have prevented a loss of meaning for many people. We owe it to people we love, self-deception being what it is, to challenge their destructive behaviors. This has to be done with humility, of course. If such confrontation ever becomes easy for us, then we will know that either caring or humility has departed.

Gentle rebuking is a biblical concept. Jesus demonstrated brave statements often. Luke 9 records many such challenges by Jesus. It makes an excellent study of the way Jesus spoke up in a conflict situation for the good of others. Here are a few examples:

"'You yourselves give them something to eat'" (v. 13 TEV, to the disciples who wanted Jesus to send the hungry crowd away).

"'For he who is least among you all is the greatest'" (v. 48 TEV, to the disciples arguing over who was the greatest; Jesus used the child by his side as an example).

"'Do not try to stop him . . . because whoever is not against you is for you'" (v. 50 TEV, to John, who was trying to stop an exorcist because he didn't belong to their group).

Encouraging Others

People who are discouraged (out of courage) need to be encouraged (to draw courage from others). I like Rollo May's simple definition: "Courage is the capacity to meet the anxiety which arises as one achieves freedom."[8]

It takes courage to seek the path of meaning rather than settle for a meaningless existence. And the courage needs to be renewed again and again. Courage is like air—we need to keep breathing it in. That is why, if we are to prevent and overcome meaninglessness, we need many more encouragers.

We can help clients gain courage by treating them *as if* they had it. If we shield and protect them, they will rightly understand that we view them as fragile. This will weaken them even further. We need to believe in "the resilient power of the human spirit." This belief of ours will help them get up once more and choose life.

If I sense clients are lacking in courage, I try to get them to spend time with young children. Little children live in a land of giants—adults who may be twice as tall as they are—so the children have to perform many acts of courage every day. If clients observe children closely, they will respect and model such courage. And they will begin to regard themselves more highly.

The woman mentioned at the beginning of this chapter who was struggling with meaninglessness and a lack of self-esteem found the courage to seek help. After counseling with a pastor for several months she wrote:

> I learned a great deal about myself, and I need to continue this learning. I'm now aware of several issues in my life that I need to deal with. I am not certain that I am entirely ready to confront all that I need to, but at least now I have a better idea of what needs to be confronted.

Because of her courage and her pastor's skills, she is slowly moving out of hopelessness, gaining some self-confidence, and discovering new directions for healing and growth.

CHAPTER TWENTY-FIVE

HELPING CLIENTS BECOME RESPONSIBLE

OFTEN WHEN PEOPLE ARE not functioning well because of emotional trauma, we take some of the load off of them. Sometimes this is a beneficial thing to do. At other times it is a mistake. The "weak" person may get the message that he is not needed, and feel like there is even less to live for. Frankl used an interesting metaphor to describe the dynamics involved here. He noted that architects, if they wish to strengthen a weak arch, increase the load on it. Thus, the parts of the arch are more firmly joined together. "So if therapists wish to foster their patients' mental health, they should not be afraid to increase that load through a reorientation toward the meaning of one's life."[1]

How can we tell who needs rest and who needs more load? If the total person is tired, if there is no energy left, then usually a rest is needed. However, if stored-up energy is there but is blocked, then they need more of a load, strategically chosen and placed. The husband of a bulimic woman had taken the load off by doing tasks she had formerly done. This resulted in her gorging and purging more. I saw them both together and helped him say what he needed to say, "I need you to do the things you used to do. You're important to this household." She needed to hear this from him. It was another reason to get well. His sincere statement helped reorient her to what was very meaningful—caring for her family.

BEING IRRESPONSIBLE

There are three levels at which one may function in terms of responsibility (see figure 8). The lowest level is irresponsibility. We either do not see what needs to be done, or if we see it, or someone tells us, we neglect or refuse to respond. Irresponsible people, if they do not change, become a growing burden to their family and to society.

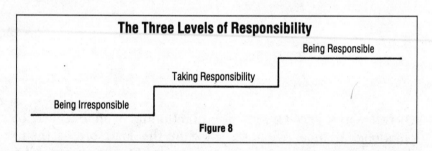

The Three Levels of Responsibility

Being Responsible

Taking Responsibility

Being Irresponsible

Figure 8

We may feel an attraction toward irresponsibility. Perhaps the source of that attraction is freedom. As we discussed earlier, the "mass neurotic triad" is made up of addiction, aggression, and depression. All three behaviors seem to offer freedom. We are free to get "a quick fix" for our emotional state, free to make someone do our will, and free to pull back from life and immobilize ourselves. We are invited to freedom, but we wake up to find ourselves in bondage. The taste of irresponsibility may be sweet at first, but the dregs are bitter.

TAKING RESPONSIBILITY

The step up to taking responsibility is a significant one. For reasons that are usually very good ones we give up some of our freedom. Someone tells us what we are to do—make a bed, do a specified amount of homework, make hamburgers in a certain way, get an engineering survey done, or "call if you're going to be home late." If we carry out the assignment, we are operating at the second level. We are responding to someone—parent, teacher, supervisor, employer, or spouse—who has some authority over us or influence with us.

Learning to take responsibility from others is important if we are going to avoid chaos at home, school, work, and in society. It is a level which we all need to reach. Functioning at this level is good—but not good enough.

BEING RESPONSIBLE

The highest level of functioning is being responsible. It is as big a step from the second level to this level as it is from the first level to the second level. A custodian who doesn't bother to pick up a piece of paper from the floor is being irresponsible. If he picks up the paper, he is *taking* responsibility. If someone else other than the custodian picks up the paper, that person is *being* responsible. Learning to differentiate between the second and third level has increased my effectiveness as a counselor.

Taking responsibility was the norm prior to World War II. Parents, teachers, and employers used to have more power by virtue of their position than they do now. The authority structure was clear in families, churches, and factories. It is much less clear today because role power has declined. To look at the trends sweeping America, as reported by John Naisbitt in *Megatrends*, is to view the decline of authority.[2] These trends include:

Industrial Society to Information Society
Centralization to Decentralization

Institutional Help to Self-Help
Representative Democracy to Participatory Democracy
Hierarchies to Networking

Since we now have fewer people giving responsibility and fewer people willing to take it, we need to help others (as well as ourselves) become responsible. How can we do this with clients?

As a family counselor I am often asked by parents, "How can I get my children to do their part of the work around the house?" So I often ask the parents to bring the entire family in so we can talk about it. These are some observations I've made about this predicament.

In some cases, the parents complaining of a lack of respect from their children are showing a lack of respect toward their children. The voice tone used on a child is similar to that which some people use on a disobedient dog. *Mutual* respect is necessary. In other situations, the parents have not done the household chores *with* the children. In those families, relationships are made to serve tasks: "You will do this because you are a member of this family!" Usually a more effective way is to make tasks serve relationships: "Let's do this together for awhile. It's more fun that way, and you can see how I go about it and decide if my method will work for you."

In many situations parents are pushing *responsibilities* rather than *responsibleness*. The teen may be functioning at level 3 at school and in her part-time job, but is rebelling at level 2 at home. I've found it useful as a family counselor to go over the three levels of responsibility with the family and ask each one at which level they see themselves functioning at work, school, and home.

A parent-training program that builds on the third level—being responsible—is "STEP: Systematic Training for Effective Parenting."[3] This program describes the "good" parent as one who insists on spoiling or shaming the child, acts self-righteous, and demands perfection, whereas the "responsible" parent believes in mutual respect, encouragement, giving choices, and setting realistic standards.[4] These behaviors and beliefs of the responsible parent help the child and adolescent to function at the top level of responsibility.

The secret of helping people of all ages become responsible is to release them to *respond to life*. One does this carefully with children, taking into account such factors as their safety. The counselor releases clients by asking Socratic questions, such as "What is life asking of you at this turning point in your journey?" or "What can *you* do to relieve the suffering of your family?" or "In this present crisis what action could you take that you could best live with ten years from now?"

CHAPTER TWENTY-SIX

EVIL AS A CAUSE OF MEANINGLESSNESS AND CONFUSION

YESTERDAY A MAN SAID in a counseling session, "My ex-wife calls me once in awhile when her new marriage is going badly. I don't like to admit it, but I'm glad when she's hurting." We then talked about the dark side of his life and why his several marriages had all ended in divorce. The client, honest and non-defensive, told how he had been unable to comfort his wives when they hurt, and how he had frequently caused them pain. Much of that pain was inflicted unintentionally, even unknowingly. As Morton Kelsey put it, "Most of the evil in this world is caused not by wicked people but by unconscious people. By the very kind of unconsciousness which lets us ignore others."[1]

The client told how much he wanted each of his wives until

the point of marriage, and then they became unimportant to him until they left him, at which point he pursued them unsuccessfully and with great mourning. He told me about his Christian experience, so we talked about the second greatest commandment, "Love your neighbor as yourself" (Mark 12:31). A spouse is probably our closest neighbor. Love here does not mean we always have a warm place in our heart for the other person, because that is not true even of ourselves. It means rather that just as we want the best for ourselves, we are to want the best for the other person.

The client freely admitted that he wanted each of the women for what they could give him. Now life had little meaning, and he craved for another woman. However, I asked him to take a year first for his own healing and growth, and for attempting to reconcile with his alienated adult children. He was angry with me, but we talked about that, and he made the decision to begin work on his spiritual life and his ability to love.

Probably all of us know what it is to want someone because we need them, rather than to love someone for what we can give them. We are more like this man than we are different from him. I think he can heal and grow because he does not try to cover up the wrong he has done. The direction for our work together is clear. As M. Scott Peck has noted, "We must know where we end and others begin."[2] This client is narcissistic enough that he at times sees others as existing to meet his own needs.

It is necessary, in counseling and in life, to call attention to evil as well as to good. We are less than honest if we do not do this. Bruno Bettelheim has observed how our "protection" of children in this regard has had dire results. We do not let children know about the reality of the evil side of humans. We lead them to believe that we are all good. But children are aware that they are sometimes bad, and even when they are good, often "they would prefer not to be. This contradicts what they are told by their parents, and therefore makes the child a monster in his own eyes."[3] If our clients know they are dealing with their dark, evil side, they at least know what they are up against.

Peck's *People of the Lie*, Kelsey's *Caring*, and Bettelheim's *The Uses of Enchantment: The Meaning and Importance of Fairy Tales* have been three useful resources for me in dealing with evil as a counselor. Peck expresses many practical insights relating to counseling those who lack meaning. For example, he notes that the evil we encounter in a client often leaves us confused. Lies, of course, cause the confusion.

Another helpful idea is that Satan's primary weapon is fear.[4] If this is true, then perhaps the primary virtue is courage. As one first-grader said when I asked him, as part of a psychological test, to define brave, "Brave is when you're scared to death but do it anyway." Yet another implication is that when clients are afraid we need to help them see reality because, as Peck points out, "Satan's threats are always empty. They are all lies."[5]

I have often not been successful in counseling where I have felt the presence of evil strongly. And in each case where this was so, I was slow in recognizing that evil was present. I tended to blame my confusion and the lack of results on my lack of ability. Also in each case, I found it difficult to terminate once I knew what was going on. Another common factor was that I felt a great sense of relief that I would not be seeing the client again, although I was very sad that I had not been useful in bringing about change. A final comment on the few situations in which I felt evil was present: I did not sense that the person who was causing the confusion and darkness *felt* any lack of meaning. This person was in each case intense, grim, and quite goal-directed.

Although there were some frightening aspects of these counseling sessions, I do not think the clear presence of evil is as dangerous as its hidden presence. Kelsey has a jarring statement about this, "If we do not love, we join the forces of the Evil One and destroy as effectively as if we were triggering a machine gun into a defenseless crowd."[6] I now do a much more effective job of discerning evil when there is darkness and confusion present. But I think evil slips up on me, and perhaps on others, when the only clue is the failure to love.

RAISING AWARENESS OF CHILDREN'S NEEDS

Children are hurt the most by our failure to love because their vulnerability renders them defenseless. Jesus emphasized the evil involved in offending a child: "'If anyone should cause one of these little ones to lose his faith in me, it would be better for that person to have a large millstone tied around his neck and be drowned in the deep sea'" (Matt. 18:6 TEV).

To prevent this great evil, we must find ways to raise awareness levels in ourselves and our clients regarding children's needs. Many adults expect children to tell them what they need. Such people do not understand childhood.

While Rudyard Kipling's parents were in India, he lived with a woman who took in children. He reported later that she and her son both regularly beat him. He looked forward each year to December, which he was allowed to spend with his aunt.

Often and often afterwards, the beloved aunt would ask me why I had never told anyone how I was being treated. Children tell little more than animals, for what comes to them they accept as eternally established.[7]

Children suffer in silence unless responsible adults observe their appearance and behavior, and infer their needs. We are carrying out the work of our Lord when we love children and reduce their suffering. We can remind clients to be gentle with children. (In our local hospital there are children who are brought to the emergency room with a dislocated shoulder. It seems a parent has lifted them by one hand and pivoted them into a car seat.) We can ask thought-provoking questions, such as "When you and your wife are fighting, what are your children feeling?" and "Have you ever experienced the fear of being abandoned?"

We can at times respond directly to suffering children. A sensitive counselor did this with a five-year-old boy she knew. When Brent was two, his father was killed in an accident. Brent's older brothers and sisters had memories of their father, but Brent did not. This was the unique aspect of his suffering. The counselor mentioned a two-year-old they both knew and said that if her daddy died, she would not remember him. This example put his situation in perspective for him so that he realized no two-year-old could be expected to remember a parent. Having dealt with his guilt she then told him of the many times she had seen his dad carry him on his shoulders and play with him. When he wanted to think of his daddy he could get out the photo album or he could go to his mom or a brother or sister and have them tell a story about him and his daddy. This memory through others would be a very special thing for him and for them. The counselor said:

He seemed to really appreciate that. When he left my house he gave me a big hug. It was like now he had something like the rest of his family to go home and build on.

COUNSELING THOSE WHO UNINTENTIONALLY HURT OTHERS

Do you know anyone who pets a cat by stroking from the tail to the head? It is possible to treat in a similar way people who love us, and we may not even know it. How do we deal with clients who are contributing to meaninglessness and confusion in the lives of those around them?

The counselor has at least three special methods available in such situations. One is the method of challenging. With the man mentioned earlier in the chapter who had hurt each of his wives, I challenged him to learn to live without a woman so that in his next relationship he could become a giver, not just a taker. Sometimes competitive people who are more inclined to a contest than a relationship will rise to a challenge. To a macho-type man who started to walk out of my counseling office when we were just getting warmed up, I said, "If you had any guts you'd come back and sit down." He came back and sat down. Although this is far from my standard practice, it was just the type of challenge my client needed to stimulate response.

A second method is a question that works like a time-release capsule. It may take effect when the client wakes up at 2:00 A.M. Often a somewhat narcissistic person going through a divorce will say "I'll make it. I'll survive." He or she is, of course, very frightened. A question might be, "How about your three-year-old?" Another question could be, "What is your wife (or husband) suffering, right now?" or "What does it mean to you when those you love are suffering?"

A third method is the use of a metaphor or story. Jesus used this method with a person who wanted to know what was involved in loving one's neighbor. In fact, Jesus used all three of these methods to call his hearers to reach out in love. By following the example of our Lord, we can confront the evil of failing to love, in ourselves and in others.

CHAPTER TWENTY-SEVEN

FINDING MEANING THROUGH CREATING

THE CREATIVE URGE within us insists that we go on living. That urge can prevent a suicide attempt. When Beethoven was thirty-two, he was anguished over his deafness. He said that there was little that kept him from ending his life. But he could not stop living with so much music within him still waiting to be expressed. He wrote, "Alas, it seems to be impossible for me to leave the world before I have done all that I feel inclined to do, and thus I drag on this miserable life."[1] Creating and living call for each other to continue.

THE SOURCE OF CREATIVITY

What is the source of creativity? There is a myth that mental illness contributes to creativity. Probably the connection between any kind of illness and creativity is not the illness itself, but the suffering that goes with it. Suffering can help provide us with a sense of the tragic in life. The sense of tragedy can then contribute clearer, more realistic outlines to whatever we create. However, the truth is that although suffering may at times enhance our creativity, it is not the source of our creativity. The source is the Creator. This truth has great relevance for the counselor.

God's first recorded act was creating. Since we are made in God's image, it follows that creating is natural and meaningful for us. The old German proverb "the clock does not strike for the happy person" certainly applies to the one who is busy creating. We lose track of time when we create. Conversely, when we are not creating, time weighs heavily upon us. My experience clinically has been that most people who are living lives that lack meaning usually have shut down their creative efforts. Their confidence, energy, and even their desire to create are lacking. If they make themselves begin to create again, their lives will often take on new meaning.

Let's suppose you have a client who lacks meaning, who used to be creative but is no longer. A first step can be Socratic questioning. "What do you do when you don't have to do anything?" "If you had the time, materials, and energy to make a special gift for someone you love, what would it be?" "What could you create that would best express you?" If, however, the client *resists* creating, then we need to look for barriers to creativity.

CONDITIONS THAT STIFLE CREATIVITY

Dr. Teresa Amabile has for many years been researching factors that encourage and discourage creativity. Her research on discouraging factors includes six methods of killing creativity:

1. Evaluating people (for example, giving employees frequent critiques of their work).
2. Watching people; surveillance (for example, a supervisor looking over an employee's shoulder).
3. Rewarding people (for example, giving out an Employee of the Month award).
4. Competition (for example, sponsoring a contest for creative ideas).

5. Restricting choice in how to do a task (for example, telling an executive not only what to do, but also how to do it, when there may be many ways to get the job done).
6. Extrinsic orientation (this is a summary of all the above methods in which the goal is to please others).[2]

A common theme in this lethal list is that people who have to spend time and energy meeting others' expectations (extrinsic motivation) have less creative energy for creating. The reason extrinsic motivation blocks creativity is that it rewards us for taking the safest, simplest route through a task. As Dr. Amabile has pointed out, the above six activities are not *always* bad. For example, we do not necessarily want assembly line workers to be creative. The emphasis there is on repetitiveness and quality control.

HELPING THE CLIENT REKINDLE CREATIVITY

It is important for the counselor dealing with the resistant, tired, non-creative client to work at *releasing* creativity rather than *directing* it. Counselor responses such as, "Why don't you try . . . ?" or "Have you thought of . . . ?" are usually not any more effective with our clients than with our children. These questions tend to heighten resistance rather than decrease it.

Conditions That Nurture Creativity

Dr. Amabile has discovered three factors that encourage creativity:
1. A high level of knowledge and experience (creativity is built on a base of facts and general information).
2. Freeing people from external motivation (as in the examples given for the methods of stifling creativity).
3. Concentrating on intrinsic motivation (such as enjoyment, personal satisfaction and interest).[3]

It may be seen by comparing the above two lists that some aspects of school, business, and daily life often involve those factors in the first list that actually kill creativity. The counselor needs to help the client be intrinsically motivated.

Sharing Creations in the Counseling Session

Because creating is an attribute of God, there is often something very spiritual about it. I frequently ask my clients to bring something to a future session which they have created in the past or will now create. They have brought amazing things—beautiful sketches and paintings, moving poems, wonderful works in wood, and creatively crafted objects. And each time as we talk about these creations together, we learn more about the client's creative urge and the relation of that urge to his or her meaning in life. Some have brought a poem or a song written by someone else that spoke deeply to them about life.

The counselor can most effectively nourish the client's creativity by sensing and encouraging the direction of the creative urge, noted above. When we create something, we "reach beyond our own death."[4] When we create something that has the potential of lasting beyond our own lives on this earth, the creative act naturally is fraught with anxiety, and thus requires courage. Perhaps one of the reasons we can construct an elaborate sand castle on the beach with little anxiety is that we know that it will not survive the next tide.

We encourage by challenging clients to use their gifts in their own unique ways. A study of clients' learning styles is useful in this regard. Some clients can express their feelings through the talk-listen mode traditionally used in counseling. Others may create a poem, sketch, or wood-form that reveals a very deep feeling or an as-yet-unexpressed meaning in their lives.

Prescribing Client Time with Children

"And what is imagination really? It is play—playing with ideas."[5] Thus Ashley Montagu emphasized in his releasing book, *Growing Young,* the relationship of creativity and play, inasmuch as imagination is an important component of creativity. Children have been helpful to me personally in releasing my own creativity. I have spent a great deal of time in the last five years with my grandchildren, served as assistant teacher with a church school class of four-year-olds (cleaned up the glue, played my guitar, and led the singing), and in many other ways spent eye-level time with little children. These have been my most creative years thus far. And I believe there is a connection.

I have asked many adults to respond to this question: "Tell about a significant time you spent with a child. At the end of your story, tell what, if anything, you learned from the child." Scores of these stories involved learning to be more released, and/or more creative.

My favorite story on creativity is this one:

My neighbor boy placed himself on his rolling horse and came riding into the kitchen. He went to the corner where he could open two cabinet doors so they touched back to back, creating a stall for a bronco. He would slam open the "gates," as it were, and ride the horse to the middle of the kitchen until he was bucked off. He figured out how to do this at a year-and-a-half by watching rodeos on TV. I was impressed at how creative he could be.[6]

This was an amazing creative act, given a small child with limited resources, living in a world of giants. We need to "prescribe" time, for our non-creating clients, with children like this. We do not need to tell these clients to learn vulnerability, creativity, or how to be released during these times. Rather, the following simple directions will be more useful: "Get down on eye level and play with them. Be as relaxed and as unhurried as you can." During the next counseling session you can help them surface what they learned. Ask your clients what evidences of creativity they observed in the child. Then do a Socratic dialogue about how the clients might release some creative acts of their own. As Walt Whitman suggested, we need to "learn from the simple—teach the wise."[7]

Invite Your Clients to Adopt an Attitude of Lifelong Learning

People cannot create without knowledge. And only a fraction of what we need to know to be creative is learned in school.

The book *Invitation to Lifelong Learning* explores "the great tradition" of continuing to learn after school is behind us.[8] The book contains over twenty-five success stories and points of view concerning lifelong learning from such creative people as Benjamin Franklin, Mortimer Adler, and Buckminster Fuller.

Some clients have stopped learning because they are in despair. A way for them to regain meaning in life is to begin nourishing themselves intellectually and spiritually by embarking on a lifelong learning plan. The Self-Directed Learning Project can be the first specific step.[9]

CHAPTER TWENTY-EIGHT

HUMOR—A TOOL TO USE IN THE DISCOVERY OF MEANING

I HAVE SEEN CHILDREN as master teachers for many years. A college student who knew of my interest in learning from children told me a story of a meaningful ride with his son, a story about the horn that was stuck.

The young dad and his two-year-old son were driving home in their pickup after having a mechanic repair the steering column. The dad glanced down and said, "That horn button looks like it's at a funny angle." He tried to straighten it, and it jumped right out of the steering column into his hand.

And the horn began honking LOUDLY! It was stuck.

The traffic was rush-hour, bumper-to-bumper. The dad was flustered, panicked, embarrassed. Most of all he wondered what to do. Then he turned and saw looking up at him a little round face which was being taken over first by a huge grin, then a laugh bubbling up from way down deep.

"My embarrassment melted away, and then I, too, could see the humor in the situation," he recalled. "I laughed at myself—and together we had a great father-son laugh. It was the most fun ride home we've had in a long time!"

After this dad told me the story, I thought about stuck horns for awhile. It's happened to me a couple of times. Next time— I'll know what to do.

It takes some of the fun out of humor to analyze it. But, at the risk of doing that, let's take a look at this incident from the point of view of the four steps of logotherapy.

First, humor helped the dad to distance from his symptoms. The symptoms were embarrassment, panic, and to some degree immobilization (he didn't know what to do). He had been hyperreflected on his predicament. The method of distancing was dereflection.

The second step is to change one's attitudes. He did this rapidly and dramatically. Through the example of his small son, his attitude changed from "A honking horn is a dreadful thing," to "A honking horn is really a riot!"

The third step is the reduction or disappearance of the symptoms. Well, the two-year-old counselor should get a medal for this one. The embarrassment, panic, and immobilization disappeared—and they didn't return!

The fourth step is an attempt, as Fabry explains it, "to secure the patient's mental health for the future."[1] My own belief is that before this young psychotherapist terminated his counseling at the end of the trip, he helped equip his father for similar trials ahead.

To assure continued bumping of my funny bone, I subscribe to *Laughing Matters,* a quarterly edited by Dr. Joel Goodman.[2] Goodman usually leads off with an interview of someone who has contributed to humor, such as cartoonist Bil Keane, Norman Cousins, or Charles Schulz.

Little posters or sayings can be useful in one's counseling office. I have had a calligrapher do several for me which I have framed, and change from time to time. One of them is an attempt to dereflect clients from revenge symptoms:

To err is human.
To forgive is . . .
Out of the question!
Another one is to help couples understand what happens after marriage. It's a two-liner from an old country western song.
I can't adjust to the you
That's adjusted to me.

HUMOR AS AN AID TO CHOOSING

Clients emerge from meaninglessness by making new choices and acting on them. They have previously made the same old choices again and again which just keep them on the treadmill of a life without meaning. Humor is one way the counselor can free them to see and act on choices they have never seen before and release their creativity. The distance from ha-ha to a-ha is a short one.

Hiroshi Takashima, a Japanese physician, uses humor in his work with patients.[3] He told of working with a fifty-six-year-old executive who was depressed. The executive felt he was growing forgetful. He connected this with aging, became worried, and went for a medical examination. A psychiatrist told him that loss of memory was a symptom of senile dementia. This frightened him even more. He went to other doctors who gave him medication and told him to take a month's vacation. His depression worsened, and he visited Dr. Takashima, who told him his company paid him an executive's salary to make judgments. His secretary was paid to remember, and it was her job to help him when he forgot things. And then Dr. Takashima used humor to distance him from his symptoms, "You should not try to memorize everything by yourself, or else your secretary will lose her job."[4] Dr. Takashima thus creatively used a "one-liner" to implement two methods of logotherapy: dereflection (to derail the executive's hyper-reflection on his forgetfulness) and paradoxical intention (to suggest that he actually not try so hard to remember). The executive left the office relieved and came back several days later to invite Dr. Takashima to dinner, saying he wanted to show the doctor he had excellent judgment in choice of restaurants, and that he would ask his secretary to remind him of the date! Dr. Takashima said regarding the diagnosis and treatment, "This is a case of a doctor-caused (iatrogenic) neurosis (pseudo-depression), which was successfully treated with logotherapy."[5]

Humor takes the terror out of a feared situation. I asked a man who had been unsuccessfully running from sleeplessness for years what would happen if one ran rapidly away from a barking dog. "Oh, the dog would run after him." I then asked if it would make a difference if the dog was a huge, salivating German shepherd or a tiny, yipping Pekinese. "No, both would run after him." By laughing at our fears, we reduce the powerful to the trivial. And though it may still "chase" us, it is no longer a threat. Whatever we laugh at loses its power over us. We need to use humor carefully, of course, so that the object of terror is ridiculed, not the client.

One of the symptoms of the client suffering from meaninglessness is grimness. The use of humor once in awhile can help the *counselor* not be likewise drowned in those joyless waters. For both counselor and client, humor has not only all the above advantages, but some additional ones resulting from chemical changes. Laughter stimulates the production of the alertness hormone catecholamine which then stimulates the release of natural painkillers, the endorphins. "Laughter, then, causes our bodies to produce our own pain killers."[6]

Finally, laughter helps us relax. We have all experienced the deep relaxation of "internal jogging" (Norman Cousins's metaphor for belly laughter). Significant learning proceeds best in a relaxed atmosphere. The appropriate use of humor in a counseling session thus promotes an atmosphere which permits long-term learning and growth.

CHAPTER TWENTY-NINE

THE MEANING OF THE MOMENT

THE QUESTION WAS A difficult one. I was training staff in caring/helping/counseling skills at a nursing home, and this was my seventh visit to this particular home over a three-year period. The question came during the last seminar of the day, which was from 1:30–2:30 A.M. with "C" shift nurses. The topic of the seminar was Counseling Those Who Have Lost Meaning in Life. Most of these nurses and aides worked in a special unit with a unique set of residents: Nearly all were suffering from memory loss and were disoriented. Some had Alzheimer's disease, others lacked memory for other reasons. Many of the residents showed no signs of recognizing the staff who had cared for them for years. It was one of the nurses who asked the question, "When a resident's memory is gone, how can life have any meaning for them and how can our work with them have meaning?"

We puzzled about that for awhile. I agreed that memory must be present to connect life and to gift us with overall meaning. But there is an additional kind of meaning—the meaning of the moment. I asked the staff members at the seminar to remember the times their mothers had diapered, fed, and kissed them when they were one or two years old. None could remember those very significant acts. Did that inability to remember the acts mean that those acts were without significance to the child or to the mother? No. Besides contributing to the development of the staff members that were there that night, those loving acts had great meaning at the moment to the child and to the mother.

The meaning of the moment comes at that instant when an act of love is given and received. So the giving of a glass of cold water, even if (especially if) offered to an elderly man with Alzheimer's disease, is taken note of by the Lord. And God remembers, although the giver and resident may not. Both the giver and the receiver are changed in some way by that act of love, even if they do not remember it two weeks or even five seconds later.

The phrase "the meaning of the moment" has an additional connotation. Imagine two or three or more people together. Let us say they have functional memories. Then something happens in that small group. One of them realizes that this something has great significance. But perhaps the others miss the meaning of what is happening.

Jesus walked the Emmaus road with two disciples after his resurrection. The disciples missed the meaning of the moment. But something happened when he sat at the table with them later, gave thanks, and broke bread.

Then their eyes were opened and they recognized him, and he disappeared from their sight. They asked each other, "Were not our hearts burning within us while he talked with us on the road and opened the Scriptures to us?" (Luke 24:31, 32 NIV).

So while they missed the moment cognitively, they did not miss it with their hearts. That can give us hope. If we cannot grasp the meaning of the moment in our minds because of being too young or too old or because of memory loss, there is still the potential that our hearts will seize the meaning of the moment. How can we help our clients sense, understand, and be emotionally aware of the meaning of the moment?

SOME OPPORTUNITIES KNOCK ONLY ONCE

At times, counseling is like careening around blind corners at full speed. We had better be able to react fast when we find out what we are facing. The choice is always dependent on the meaning of the situation, or, in some cases, the moment. Rollo May has reported that Kierkegaard used the term *augenblick* to refer to "the pregnant moment."[1] The term literally translated means "the blinking of an eye." "It is the moment when a person suddenly grasps the meaning of some important event in the past or future. . . . "[2] Awareness is heightened and there is a sudden insight.

This same concept is denoted by the Greek word *kairos,* one of the New Testament words for time. It is used to signify a seasonable time, a fixed period, or "this time." An example of this use is Galatians 6:10, "Therefore, as we have the opportunity, let us do good to all people, especially to those who belong to the family of believers." An opportunity comes and goes, and we either grasp it and act on it, or we don't. This is why the focus in counseling should be on what is happening at this moment (*augenblick*) rather than on techniques. As the counselor attends to the present moment, the client learns by example to do the same. Hopefully this client behavior will generalize beyond the counseling office, so that opportunities will be seized as life presents them.

THE DISCUSSION OF VALUES

We are all committed to a number of values even though we might not be able to name them all. By using Socratic questioning, the counselor can help clients clarify their values. Those values that work against meaning in life can be challenged by the counselor. Sometimes a client will talk about falling out of love, and will place comfort or pleasure above commitment. If clients choose not to honor marriage vows, I challenge them on the worth of their promise at the time of the wedding. Now, there may be sufficient reason to renounce a vow, such as a spouse's infidelity. If that happens, the client needs to make a tragic moral choice, that is, choose the lesser wrong—violate a promise, or allow the partner to continue to violate the marriage by unfaithfulness. But just not feeling like loving the spouse for a month or even a year is an insufficient reason to bail out of a marriage. We have probably gone that long at times without liking ourselves.

We grasp the meaning of the moment through the eyes of our value system. A strong value system is a good safeguard against impulsive action. It is also an effective safeguard against passivity when confronted by injustice being done to others. I have asked clients to write out a list of "I believe" statements and bring it to the next session for discussion. One of my discoveries is that many people are living by someone else's beliefs.

GUIDELINES FOR SENSING THE MEANING OF THE MOMENT

1. Adopt the point of view, "The present moment is an unrepeatable miracle." I have had this saying framed and on my desk for a number of years. Miracles are real. Many of them are repeatable. But the present moment is a miracle that cannot be repeated.

2. Tune in to your senses. What are you hearing? A bird singing? What about another's voice? Is there a quivering of fear? The sound of celebration, joy, or sadness? What are you seeing? What does the other person's stance or posture tell you? What message comes from the eyes?

3. What emotions are you feeling at the moment? Do you feel love or hate—or both? Is there anger or contentment? Take time to be aware of how you feel.

CREATING PEAK EXPERIENCES

We have all had special moments—peak experiences. They left us transformed in some way, whether it was a renewal, a quiet walk during which we made an important decision, listening to music, a lonely weekend when we had to face ourselves, finishing a good book, or an affirmation from a friend that revitalized our confidence. They are so healing and growth-producing that I've often wondered if we can *make* them happen. I have concluded that at least we can create an atmosphere that is conducive to peak experiences. One way is by telling the truth.

Honesty

If a peak experience happens, it is in an honest setting. The counselor mirrors reality. A client said to me recently, "I would have killed myself, but I didn't have the courage." I replied, "No, it was not the lack of courage that kept you from picking up the handgun. It takes more courage to keep on living when you are suffering than it does to shoot yourself. The real reason you didn't take the gun in your hand was love—your love for your family."

Telling him the truth was a challenge to keep on living. He was thinking, incorrectly, that he had chosen the coward's way out—not killing himself. With this attitude he might again attempt suicide when he thought he was feeling "brave." I think my honest response was a bit of a peak experience for him. He perhaps learned that he had no right to waste his life. It was not his own to throw away.

A Sense of Adventure

I always thought that it was too bad that fairy tales did not keep going after the last line: " . . . and they lived happily forever after." However, if they had continued, I wouldn't have read them anyway because the drama was past, the challenge was over. If we were doing a graph of the amount of adventure present, the line would have been fairly low at the words "they lived happily ever after." And that's all right. We can't live with a steady state of high excitement all our lives. But is there a way of creating a sense of adventure with a client so that the possibility of a peak experience is present in the session?

Counseling is analogous to the edge sports—sky diving, rock climbing, downhill skiing. The counselor has to make rapid decisions, and there is a lot at stake. The aim in much counseling is to get the client to make a choice, to be "response-able."

The skill of challenging is one of the chief methods in the repertoire of the counselor who seeks to help a client discover the adventure of choosing meaning in life. It is not enough to seek insight—"What do you expect from life?" We invite the client to respond to the questions that life itself is asking. This approach shows that life requires a choice and action, not just an answer.

Understanding

Frieda Fromm-Reichmann said, "The patient needs an experience, not an explanation."[3] But how are we to create a setting in which an experience grips both the client and us with a strength no explanation ever could? I have had these peak experiences both as the helper and "helpee." One person feels deeply understood by the other for the very first time ever about past suffering, and the eyes of both people fill with tears and there is a release. Something good and irreversible has happened.

Reconciliation

The peak experiences in counseling when I have most felt the presence of God have occurred when I witnessed a reconciliation of family members. Each time I have felt it was the work of the Holy Spirit. A father, mother, and teenaged daughter sat on a sofa in a counseling room. The mother said, "I'm tired of acting as a go-between for you two!" I asked if she would like to move from between them. She declined. Later in the session I asked her to move, noting that even with the most loving intentions the one in the middle not only is a go-between for two angry people, but also is actually in the way of their getting together. Still later in the session, the dad reached for his daughter and they hugged each other and cried. That experience kept me high for two weeks.

Another time a couple who had been married for fifteen years, whom I had been counseling for several months, and who had been separated for a month, showed up happy for counseling. For the first time in my office they sat close to each other. He had pulled off the road one day in his pickup, prayed, and received Christ. Then he worked to improve his listening skills. They reconciled without any human help. It was a peak experience for us to sit there and talk about God's intervention in their relationship. We were in the presence of love.

Prayer

I pray a lot for my clients, and sometimes I pray with them. Once in a while clients will ask if we can pray together. Some of these times have been very close. There have been times when I initiate prayer if I sense that the client is open to prayer and desirous of it.

CHAPTER THIRTY

INTRODUCING CLIENTS TO
INTERGENERATIONAL RESOURCES

WHILE WORKING WITH clients who could find little meaning in life, I intuitively connected them, when possible, with either little children or the elderly. A college student had overdosed, and was now looking longingly at repeating this escape attempt. Without really knowing why, I took her with me to visit a friend at a nursing home. The "match" worked, and she began visiting him on her own. A middle-aged client wanted to become less "stiff" and more spontaneous. I helped her arrange time each week to spend on "all fours" with children in a pre-school.

A forty-year-old man in family counseling was confronted by his wife and three children on his inability to play. He finally said, after a period of dawning awareness, that he had never played, even as a child. He had gone from age five to age twenty-one in one afternoon when his own father had impressed upon him the importance of work. From that point on, he did very little playing in his growing up days. He gradually adopted this "all-work-no-play" theme as his own, and was now trying to pass it on to his wife and children. They weren't buying it.

He agreed, with a bit of nudging from me, to spend an hour or so a week with his middle child building things with wood. There were two important outcomes from this: 1) He spent more time with his son, with whom he was not as involved as he was the other two children, and 2) he made one step toward learning to play. Doing a craft with a child is play that has a product. He could allow himself to play as long as he emerged with a product that was evidence that he had worked. Going from a product-orientation (work) to the process orientation of "pure" play usually requires the middle step of crafts.

THE RATIONALE FOR DOING AN
INTERGENERATIONAL MATCH

After I had done many of these matches with clients, I tried to analyze why it was working. I'm still not sure. My hunch is that God means for us to live in community with all ages. I know that I feel more whole if I have friends all the way from two years old to ninety-five years old. Also, I know from clinical observation and personal experience that there is something healing about these intergenerational connections. Life suddenly has renewed meaning after one of these experiences. A client may finally get moving again. So personally and clinically I am sure it works.

SOME IMPLICATIONS FOR COUNSELORS

If you have not utilized this resource to introduce new meaning to your clients, I invite you to give it a try. Plan some intergenerational contacts with at least five of your clients over a period of time. This will give you a large enough sample to make a judgment about its usefulness. If it proves to be a useful method, then you can go on to the next step of building a network of resource persons. You don't need to talk to them about your network. Just make note of names mentally or on paper of those you can call on in the future. Doing this may enlarge your own list of friends of all ages.

Some people have access to many children. Others know very few as friends. There are many ways of making friends with kids that are usually effective. One is to sit on the front porch instead of the patio in the evenings. Another is to get down on your knees and talk with at least two small children before or after worship service each week.

Many clients have children of their own at home. An anxious, panicked client was searching for peace and joy. I talked with him about his four-year-old and two-year-old. It was the first time he smiled during that session. He said he had been too busy to play with his children recently. I told him that I agreed that he was very busy, and that he reminded me of the carpenter who was too busy to sharpen his saw. Here he was desperately seeking joy and peace, and he had two "in-house" master teachers of those subjects just waiting for him to come to class! He decided he could take a little time to go to school.

College students respond very well to a match with children or an elderly person. Many college students live in residence halls with hundreds of other nineteen-year-olds, and thus lack a sense of the unity of life. Scores of my college students have chosen to visit a grandparent or a nursing home resident as their Self-Directed Learning Project. They often forge a bond so strong that it lasts far beyond the college semester. In each situation, it has expanded the life meaning of both the student and the older adult. In a Christian campus group, for which I serve as college advisor, we have had matches that have lasted as long as ten years. In choosing an older person it is useful to find someone whose life is filled with meaning. This person can then serve as a model, or perhaps even a mentor, in your client's own journey toward meaning.

I have found some clients are more open to a match with a child, and others more open to a match with an elderly person. Recently a seventeen-year-old client said she didn't like kids, but she enjoyed spending more time with her grandmother. She began, for the first time, to listen to her grandmother talk about her life experiences. This dereflection process helped draw the adolescent out of a preoccupation with her own world, and the experience expanded her meaning in life.

BEYOND WORDS

Sometimes it is not enough for the counselor just to talk or even listen to the client who lacks meaning in life. The client may need an experience rather than words. To recommend such an experience, the counselor needs to figure out the nature of the meaninglessness. Usually the client is not responding to what life is asking of him or her, or feels cut off in some way from life. Using intergenerational resources—matching the client with a child or older person—is powerful because it can help meet both those needs. There is now a task to be accomplished—regular visits—and a new connection with life.

Why the very young and the very old? Client matches with the two extremes of life are especially useful because little children and the elderly are honest, and because they usually have time for people. Dennis Benson and Stan Stewart have written about the ministry of children.[1] They use the term "Starchildren" to refer to children because "they come to us red-hot from the heart of God."[2] In a real sense we are in the presence of God when we are with a child, especially a little child. The creative act of God that brought the child into the world is so fresh that perhaps part of the meaning of that new life gives us fresh hope and renewed meaning.

What is special about the elderly? They are closer to death than the rest of us. As someone has said, "The thought of death trivializes trivia." Many elderly rejoice in the fact that they know better now than to worry about the things in life that once loomed large.

Finally, both the young and the old are excellent models of the relational theology of the Bible. The young are not able to do tasks yet and the very old are no longer able to do them. But both find the center of their meaning in deepening the relationships with those they love and who love them.

CHAPTER THIRTY-ONE

THE MEANING OF TOUCH

DESCARTES' RATIONALISTIC doctrine, "I think, therefore I am," set the stage for a mind-body dualism and for a kind of isolationism. We can think by ourselves—only by ourselves. Perhaps this rationalism that Descartes fostered accounts for Ashley Montagu's contention that the Western world relies primarily on the "distance senses" (sight and hearing) for communication, rather than the "proximity senses" (taste, smell, and touch).[1] Thus, "He can reach out to other planets, but too often he cannot reach out to his fellowman."[2] This isolation has contributed to a "disconnectedness," and therefore to a lessening of meaning in life.

MEANING AND TOUCH

The fact that touch has great meaning has been demonstrated by its impact on physical well-being. Therapeutic touch is touch given with compassion and with the intent to heal. It was discovered by Dolores Krieger in 1975 and is increasingly used in nursing.[3] Pilot studies have been done in which therapeutic touch was used as a primary method of treatment with small groups of elderly people over a five-year period. Such touch was found to be associated with the prevention of decubitus ulcers (bed sores), to reduce the inflammation, joint-swelling, and pain associated with arthritis, and to reduce spasticity and pain in stroke patients. Since it heals and nourishes, it is a small wonder that touch has been referred to as "the mother of the senses."[4]

The meaning of touch is made clear in Hermann Hesse's little book *Siddhartha*.[5] Siddhartha grew up the son of a Brahmin, and enjoyed the close friendship of Govinda. The two young men left their homes and went through many experiences together and separately trying without success to quench their thirst for meaning—and peace. Near the end of his life, Siddhartha joined an old ferryman and helped take people back and forth across the river, learning "that love is the most important thing in the world."[6] He found peace. Govinda came to the river, still searching. The two men, now old, talked. Govinda asked for something to help him on his way. Siddhartha told him to kiss him on the forehead. In that kiss—that touch—Govinda was suddenly connected with all of life. "Incontrollable tears trickled down his old face. He was overwhelmed by a feeling of great love. . . . "[7]

Most people have experienced a touch, a kiss, a hug that has released the tears of suffering and joy, and has connected them with life. It is the power of the proximity sense of touch to release and connect that brings meaning when the distance senses of sight and hearing do not. Sometimes people have to provide their own touch. Several years ago I was talking with a ninety-three-year-old woman who lived alone. I noticed she ran her forefinger back and forth across her lower lip. I wondered why she did this and then realized she was giving herself touch. Both the fingertip and lip are very sensitive, and the stimulation of this touch was important to her.

Touch must mean a great deal because some children will misbehave just to get touched (harshly) by their parents. It seems incredible that children would prefer a spanking to no touch at all. But many family counselors can verify that this happens.

COUNSELOR-CLIENT TOUCH

"We live in a strange time when it is perfectly acceptable to induce convulsions in a person with electricity, yet it may be illegal to hold that same person's hand."[8] Thus Dr. Jules Older has described the counselor's predicament in his excellent book, *Touching Is Healing.* Montagu has noted that, despite the value of counselor-client touch, "nevertheless, to this day psychoanalysts in the English-speaking world at least desist from so much as shaking hands at the beginning and end of each hour."[9] He notes that the reason given for not shaking hands is "that it would be introducing into the analytic situation an unnecessary and hence unwelcome psychic stimulus. . . . "[10]

What is the *meaning* of touch? Meaninglessness is the result of being disconnected with life. Touch reconnects us. Therefore, touch can have instant, and strong, meaning. Even the counselor-client handshake can have meaning, because "in the handshake something immediate and direct is told us about the other person. . . . "[11] It is the beginning of the discovery process.

Should counselor-client touch go beyond the handshake? Each counselor has to find his or her own way here. I have, on occasion, hugged clients, both men and women. Sometimes they have initiated it. Sometimes I have. For me such touch needs to be both *spontaneous* and morally *right.* There have been a few seductive clients who have wanted to be held, or even cuddled on my lap. I refused because I felt this touch would have been morally wrong. Touch is risky enough without violating one's intuition.

I have worked with families in my small office in which I used touch as a way to direct the conversational traffic. By sitting next to the "long talker" in a family a counselor can, with a slight touch, help that person defer to a family member who rarely gets the chance to speak. On the other hand, a slight touch can be an encouragement to talk.

The best precautionary guidelines I have seen regarding

counselor touch are those given by Jules Older. He gives five reasons *not* to touch a client:

1. Because you don't want to.
2. Because you sense the patient doesn't want you to.
3. Because, although you want to and sense the patient wants you to, you do not feel that this is the most effective therapeutic maneuver.
4. Because you feel you are being manipulated, conned, or coerced into a touch.
5. Because you suspect that you are going to manipulate, con, or coerce the patient by your touch.[12]

TEACHING CLIENTS ABOUT TOUCH

I have attempted to help many clients to become reconnected with the people in their world through touch. With a distanced couple it may be a prescription to hold each other three minutes a day. With a parent couple in a non-touching family I may teach them to give each other a gentle shoulder and back rub at the regathering time at the end of the day. Their children will observe this and often want to be a part of it. Sometimes a father who isn't ready to give or receive rubs or hugs can be helped to get in touch with his family in other ways. He can put his hands on his boy's shoulder and say, "You're really getting broadshouldered!"

The touch-training with parents by a counselor can have very positive influences on the next generation. Montagu has noted that the rough way in which many men handle women and children indicates their parents may have failed them in their own early touch experience.[13] There are many evidences that if we are touched gently as children, we will be more likely to touch our own family members tenderly as adults. We need to help our clients discover the value of touch. Then they will find their own ways to touch. As Older has noted, "Touching is not a technique: Not touching is a technique."[14]

CHAPTER THIRTY-TWO

TERMINATING COUNSELING—THE MEANING OF LEAVING

HENRI NOUWEN HAS SAID, "The words of Jesus: 'It is for your good that I leave,' should be a part of every pastoral call we make. We have to learn to leave so that the Spirit can come."[1] I believe these words apply also to us as counselors, whether or not we are pastors.

I have found that the leaving is usually painful, both for the client and the counselor. Usually clients initiate the termination process when they no longer need my help to "make it." If they do not, I initiate it when the time seems right to me. However, I have noticed that sometimes I have resisted their initiative to end the counseling, and sometimes they have resisted mine. When we talk about this, we have often discovered that one or both of us is suffering from separation anxiety. Counseling involves a friendship and it is difficult to visualize not spending time in the future together talking about things that matter. Even for the pastor who will continue to see the parishioner-client in church activities, the relationship will not be quite the same.

GUIDELINES FOR TERMINATION

1. It is useful to "taper off" rather than abruptly stop the counseling sessions. Then the counselor can transition from less frequent sessions to an "on-call" relationship. For instance, we don't set up further sessions, but the client can call for one if there is a need. Some clients call. Most do not.

2. During the tapering-off period, it is important for the counselor to bring up three areas for discussion, in addition to responding to any concerns of the client. These include:

a. The reorientation of the client to meaning, now that the undesirable symptoms have diminished or disappeared. Specific guidelines for this important step of logotherapy are given following the general guidelines for termination.

b. The separation anxiety that is a part of most leaving. John Bowlby has noted that anxiety and anger come from the same common root word, *angst,* and that the helper should be prepared to deal with both emotions when there is a separation for any reason.[2] Working through these emotions and the natural causes for them is a useful part of termination. The presence of separation anxiety is an affirmation of the investment and friendship that have been such an important part in making the counseling session effective.

c. The spiritual meaning of leaving, if the client is open to spiritual resources. Nouwen speaks of such leaving as a "creative withdrawal."[3] The memory of the sessions can perhaps become as important as the sessions themselves. If we had not had close, painful, joyous times together, the leaving would have no meaning. But having been together, we can learn to separate in such a way that the Spirit can come. Thus we can be remembered by the client "as a living witness of God. This shows the importance of being sensitive to the last words we speak before we leave a room or house; it also puts the possibility of a prayer before leaving into a new light."[4]

"Leaving" somehow sounds more human, as well as spiritual, than "terminating" the counseling. It is more human because whereas termination is usually done unilaterally by the counselor, taking leave is decided upon jointly by counselor and client. It is more spiritual because termination has the sound of permanence whereas leaving can be a temporary condition, and as Christians we know that we will be meeting again.

The client, no longer seeing the counselor regularly, will develop a new sense of responsibility, and a new reliance on the Holy Spirit. If the counselor is careful to deal with any dependency prior to the ending of counseling, this responsibility will develop much faster than it otherwise would.

GUIDELINES FOR REORIENTATION OF THE CLIENT TO MEANING

Let us suppose that the counseling has been effective and the first three steps of logotherapy have been completed: 1) helping your client distance from symptoms; 2) bringing about attitudinal change; and 3) the actual reduction or disappearance of the symptoms. The overall result is that the client no longer is combatting meaninglessness each day. In the last stage of counseling, the question is, "How can the counselor assist the client to prepare for a new, symptomless life?"

BECOMING RESPONSIBLE

One of the "advantages" of struggling with meaninglessness, and losing, is that we don't have to respond to life. We are too busy responding to our own struggle. Once we discover meaning in our lives a new vista opens to us. The view is delightful, but may also be alarming. In a counseling group I led many years ago in junior high school, one of the seventh graders had his life together and knew what school was for—learning. One of the other seventh grade boys said to him, "We'd like you better if you didn't get such good grades." There is often a price to be paid when we begin to respond to life. I asked the boy during the group session if he planned to continue to learn well, despite the price of not being fully accepted by the other boys. Also we began to talk in the group about the bases for friendship. Can we only allow people to be friends who do not excel us in any way? We become responsible by doing the best we can at a task. Becoming responsible also involves accepting others' response to life in a non-competitive way.

EXPANDING THE MEANING HORIZON

Let us suppose that a client has found new meaning in her life by recareering at age thirty-five. She had lost her former job because of a reduction in force. Even though the job was boring for her, she was overcome with despair because she was not able to find other employment. She chose to go back to college and prepare for a career she had "always dreamed about." She no longer experiences the meaninglessness of an unfulfilling job. She now has a career that is satisfying and has a bright future.

But that is not enough. This client needs help to look for fulfilling opportunities apart from her job. What else is life asking from her? If she can develop several significant values in her life—family, friends, volunteer work, creativity—she will be much less likely to be plunged into despair again because of the loss of a single value, whether that value is a job or a friend.

ATTENDING TO SPIRITUAL GROWTH

A final area to check is the client's spiritual life. One example of a Socratic question here is, "How would you rate your spiritual life along a line from 1 to 10, where 1 represents a vast distance between you and God, and 10 represents a close, loving relationship?" It is important to discuss spiritual life and growth at the end of counseling even if we have talked often of spiritual matters in earlier sessions.

PART THREE

THE COUNSELOR'S USE OF SELF

ARTHUR COMBS HAS supported eloquently the view of "self as instrument" in counseling.[1] He has noted that a common characteristic of the helping professions is *"instantaneous response."*[2] The teacher, the nurse, the counselor, the pastor, and the social worker are all expected to respond immediately. Therefore, "Professional helpers must be thinking, problem-solving people; the primary tool with which they work is themselves."[3]

This point of view is most applicable in the approach that dealing with meaninglessness requires. Rollo May has explained the significance of the "presence" of the counselor as "the therapist being not merely a shadowy reflector but an alive human being. . . . "[4] In addition to asking themselves, "What kind of skills does this counselor have?" potential clients also ask, "What kind of *person* is this to whom I will be entrusting my thoughts?" Therefore, we need to continually attend to our own healing and growth.

CHAPTER THIRTY-THREE

RECEIVING FROM CLIENTS

MORTON KELSEY SAID that listening to the anguish of others stirs up our own. He noted that "Jung listened to so much darkness that he found it necessary to go away one month in four in order to discharge the poison he had picked up in listening."[1] This example, plus other evidences that all counselors could give, provide one solid reason for continuing our own healing and growth—we are being constantly drained as counselors. If we don't continue our own search for meaning, we'll soon be empty. Another important reason for continuing the search is the concept of "self-as-instrument" in counseling, noted earlier. More important than the techniques he or she brings to the session is the kind of person the counselor is (although methods and techniques are very important). This concept is particularly relevant to counseling for meaning which depends heavily on the depth of the interpersonal encounter of client and counselor. Since we are an "instrument" in counseling, we need to continue our growth process so we will be as good as we can be.

Admittedly, counseling drains us. Therefore, we need constant renewal. How can we program renewal experiences for ourselves? One resource is often overlooked—the clients themselves. We can receive from them as well as give to them. But we need to be willing and intentional about this. I have worked with professionals in the human services for a long time. About ten or fifteen years ago I began to notice an emerging pattern. Professionals in this area—such as teachers, pastors, and nurses—are usually excellent givers but poor receivers. Nearly all of our training focuses on giving, and it's easy to forget about our very human need to receive. At this point we become dispensers, very professional but not very human. If it is more blessed to give than receive, we should permit our clients to receive this blessing of giving even during the session. How can the counselor receive as well as give? I have been intentionally receiving from my clients the last ten years, and have discovered some clues.

RECEIVING FROM THOSE WHO ARE SUFFERING

I know from working ten years as a volunteer with a community personal crisis telephone service and almost two years with hospice that even a relatively small city has an immense amount of human suffering. I regard counseling as a part of my mission to reduce suffering, and that has great meaning for me. This involves giving, of course. And yet it is from those who are suffering the most that I have received the most unexpected gifts. A Viet Nam veteran who lost his wife to a tragic accident came for family counseling with his three children. They were struggling together to find meaning and to come to terms with their grief. There was a beauty about that family that touched me deeply. I think it was their commitment to each other that was a legacy from the wife-mother whom I had never met. It showed me the amazing impact that one person can have on a family.

At the end of the second counseling session with a couple, the man asked me, "How do you keep on doing what you do when people dump on you all the time?" I thought about it for awhile and said I didn't really see that I had been dumped on during these two sessions, but rather that they had shared their sufferings. And I agreed with his point that it did something to me. It took something out of me. On the other hand, I had received from them. He had a dry sense of humor that relaxed me, and his wife had an awareness of what was going on in the session that helped me. One time she had said to me, "You're angry!" I thought, "Ha! She's telling me, the counselor, that I'm angry, when I'm cool and rational?" Then I realized I was angry, admitted it, thanked her for bringing me back to the real world, and we continued.

RECEIVING FROM THOSE WHO ARE VULNERABLE

I sat with a mom and dad and their ten-year-old daughter as they shared. There was a lot at stake, and I was quite apprehensive in beginning the session. I didn't admit it—I tried to act cool and professional. It was a good session, thanks to the girl's insights. At one point she said, "I think we just need to try a little harder and talk about our feelings." At the end, after I had "closed" the session, she held up her hand and said, "Can I talk about my feelings before coming here today?" I nodded. "I was scared. I didn't know what family counseling was. I decided I wouldn't talk—but I did. I feel OK now." I thanked her for telling how she had felt, and said I had been scared, too, but hadn't shared my feelings like she did. And I told her that her example would help me to be more honest in the future. I suddenly realized in a fresh way how much it meant for someone to break through the barriers and be honest.

Most people who seek counseling have a certain vulnerability that is a good model for me. I think it comes from their suffering and their openness to receive help for it. Their defenses are down, so "what you see is what you get." Because of their suffering, they have gone beyond the pretense that insulates many of us from each other. A good example of a vulnerable person is the little girl mentioned above. She did not exhibit any defenses during the session.

RECEIVING SPIRITUAL STRENGTH AND INSIGHT

The client gift that has the most meaning to me in terms of my own healing and growth is the spiritual kinship I feel with many of my clients. I know many are as interested in my own spiritual growth as I am in theirs. Quite a few tell me that they pray for me. I have worked with couples who are experiencing great pain and anger in their relationship, yet there is a spiritual kinship that unites them, and connects them with me. It is this kinship that keeps them together. And it is this kinship that allows me to confront and challenge them without damaging the counseling relationship. Finally, it is this kinship that renews my own strength.

CHAPTER THIRTY-FOUR

THE PASTOR'S TWO FAMILIES

A NUMBER OF PASTORS' wives have said to me in a counseling session, "My husband has another lover—the church!" Indeed, the pastor is probably the only professional with two legitimate families. Some other professionals almost have two families: coaches and their athletes, doctors and their patients, kindergarten teachers and their students—in these relationships there is often a sense of closeness and caring that approaches that of a family. But the church *is* a family—the family of God. And the New Testament is clear that God's family will continue into eternity, although the structure of the earthly family will not.

I bring up the subject of the pastor's two families because many pastors will be using these Resources for Christian

Counseling. In addition, those who are reading this who are not pastors will perhaps thus be able to be even more understanding and supportive of pastors.

I went to seminary for graduate rather than professional education because I was not preparing to be a pastor, and therefore was not ordained at the end of the three years. I planned to teach in a Christian school or college, but instead have worked in public schools and colleges for nearly thirty years. The seminary training was helpful to me in understanding the theology of the pastor's role. Also, for eighteen years now, I have been leading counseling workshops for pastors, and serving as advisor to pastors in graduate programs. Many of the workshops have included pastors' spouses. I like to do seminars and workshops that help unite rather than divide pastoral couples. These workshop experiences with pastors of all major denominations and many smaller denominations have helped me understand the pulling and tearing that goes on when the spouse and children are hanging onto one arm of the pastor and the church members are pulling on the other. A similar situation occurs with Roman Catholic priests and single Protestant pastors, because they have a family of origin that loves them and needs them.

PRIORITIES

Which family should have the priority? I led a two-day workshop several years ago for pastors and spouses with about two hundred and fifty in attendance. This workshop preceded the national convention of the denomination, so I stayed and attended the convention. During the convention quite a number of pastors made appointments to talk with me, as did several spouses. The men all talked about church problems while the women all talked about family problems. So, it sometimes makes a difference with whom one talks as to which family should receive priority.

Certainly the Bible is clear that our number one priority is our relationship with God. That is not in question. The question is, "Which *family* should get the priority?" Only each individual pastor can answer this question, of course, but I want to make some suggestions about the importance of spouse and children. These suggestions come out of nearly twenty years of counseling families—many of them pastors' families.

One thought is that it is important to listen to older pastors talk about their priorities. Morton Kelsey, an Episcopal priest, is quite strong and eloquent concerning his point of view: "If I had one thing to do over in life with regard to my loving and my listening, I would have clarified my priorities and placed my wife and my children at the top of the list. God has given me these special people as primary objects for care and love."[1]

One of the difficulties that pastors' families face is that many pastors never go off duty, at least in their own minds. I called a pastor at his home about 10:00 P.M. and he answered, "Pastor Smith speaking." Later I asked him when he went off duty. There were a number of persons other than parishioners who could have been calling him, such as friends, neighbors, parents, and siblings, yet the pastor's role was uppermost in his mind.

CLARIFYING AND COMMUNICATING PRIORITIES

Many pastors use a checklist or other type of evaluation form to clarify for themselves and their parishioners which tasks should receive priority. Usually there are several general headings, such as pastoral ministry, worship, Christian education, administration, ministry to the community, and pastoral development. Pastoral ministry would include crisis work, evangelism, youth ministry, and so forth. It works best for each pastor and pastoral relations committee to make up their own form so that their particular concerns are reflected, or to modify or add to a form suggested or required by a denomination.

If your church has a total of twenty tasks that they see as required of their pastor, then board members and other interested members could be asked to rank order these tasks from 1 to 20, with 1 being most important and 20 least (but still) important. One advantage of this ranking process is that church members have to struggle with priorities and thereby will better understand the difficult choices facing their pastor.

It is good to include under the pastoral development heading an item entitled Spending Quality and Quantity Time with the

Pastor's Own Family. What ranking will members give to this task of the pastor? What ranking will the pastor give it? After the pastor has rank-ordered the tasks, then the members' and the pastor's ranking can be compared. If the pastor ranks time with family very high, this sends an important and clarifying signal to the congregation. And this high ranking can benefit the entire church, because church members need their pastors to model strong, effective family life.

As pastors take a stand to strengthen their own personal families, there will be a ripple effect in the church. Pastors are saying by their action, "My family is very high on the list of my priorities." And pastors will need the affirmation and support of the rest of us as they make this commitment and implement it. Pastors who make this choice will then feel a greater sense of integrity as they work with couples and families in their church.

CHAPTER THIRTY-FIVE

JOINING YOUR CLIENT

I KNEW FROM THE father's call that the first family counseling session would not be an easy one. The IC (Identified Client) was eighteen years old and rebelling against most of the things her folks believed. Besides her and her parents, an older sister and a younger brother would be coming. It is difficult to connect with one client during the first session, much harder to connect with two in marriage counseling, and a tremendous challenge to connect with each of five people in a family, especially with ages ranging from twelve to forty. After greeting each of the five with a smile, eye contact, and a handshake, I played a carefully chosen song on my cassette recorder—"Perhaps Love," sung by Placido Domingo and John Denver.[1]

It is a song that gives many definitions of love. I asked the family members to note which definition sounded right to them. The music was unexpected and calming. It gave the six of us something common on which to focus. Then we each told what we identified with in the song. It then seemed a natural step to look at the love in their family and the barriers that were up right now that were keeping them from expressing their love.

Touch, eye contact, and music help the counselor join clients in another way. Some clients are in the past time zone (perhaps regretting), some are in the future (probably fearing), and some are in the present. Music is a resource that helps bring people into the present. The counselor and client need to be in the same time zone if they are to connect.

RESPECTING HUMAN DIGNITY

An important way I have found to join clients is to respect their dignity as human beings. This respect touches something very deep inside people and usually permits a bridge of trust to be built rapidly. The biggest barrier to connecting is fear. When clients sense from a counselor that their dignity is being respected, they understand that they will not be misused and the trust that results allows them to relax.

The roots of the respect for human dignity are deeply embedded in spiritual ground. Each person is a unique creation of God. Treating clients from this point of reference helps us avoid iatrogenic damage (injury caused by the care giver). Iatrogenic damage is a significant concern of most experienced counselors. One reason for this is the recent sharp rise in the number of law-suits against human service professionals, including ministers, psychologists, and others who do counseling. A deeper reason is a genuine caring by these counselors for their clients, coupled with the understanding that harm can be done easily, and often unknowingly, by a counselor.

Iatrogenic damage is most likely to occur during the early, diagnostic phase of counseling. One counselor told of a neurologist who treated a patient for confusion. He told her she had an "attack of paranoia." Medication cleared up her confusion but now many years later she is still dreading an attack of paranoia. An iatrogenic neurosis begins "with the concurrence of two factors: a careless remark or behavior by the physician, and hyperreflection by the patient."[2] The counselor needs to be very careful about the use of label words. For example, a client used the term "insomnia" for his condition. I used "sleeplessness." It is less mysterious, and therefore more manageable. Respect for our client requires that we talk about words until we have a common understanding.

This respect for the human dignity of our clients allows us to connect on the same level. Rollo May talks about the problem of some clients who "surrender their being to the therapist—which can only lead to a submerged despair, a burrowing resentment that will later burst out in self-destructiveness."[3] To avoid this I tell my clients, especially those most out of control, that I see them in control of the counseling session. It is not a vertical surgeon-patient relationship in which I am active and they are passive. It is a horizontal counselor-client relationship, in which we both need to be very active. But I am simply their consultant. Only they can discover the true meaning and mission of their lives. At this point I often use a line of integrity therapists, "You alone can do it, but you can't do it alone." The responsibility is the client's but I will walk alongside in a supportive way. I have found that people who have been sexually assaulted or have been "controlled" in other ways need to know they are in control, even if they initially resist that responsibility.

JOINING THE CLIENT'S TIME ZONE

Time zones were mentioned very briefly in the earlier reference to music. I follow two steps in joining the client in time. First, I try to get them into the present moment. This is not always easy. If they are panicked, they are usually locked into a future time frame dreading some expected event. If they are depressed or guilty they are often locked just as tightly in a past time frame. In either case I work hard to pull them into the present moment. Anything that provides a sensory experience—tea, coffee, touch, eye contact, a calm voice—helps "bring them to their senses," back to the present moment.

After I sense they are in the present moment—reality—then

I try to move with them into the time zone of their greatest concern. This is the second step in joining the client's time zone, and is done through empathy.

Key Words

Much of my book *Connecting with a Friend* is about the skills of joining a client, so I don't want to duplicate those methods here.[4] But a final method of joining needs to be explained. I listen carefully to the *words* of the client, as well as the ideas. If a word like "empty" or "worthless" is used several times, I file it in my mind and use the word in my responses. Also if the client uses terms specific to an interest area, such as sports, business, or art, I join the client by using some of the terms. For example, with a health professional I talk about the *symptoms* of meaninglessness, and a *treatment plan*. With an athlete I use terms like *goals, time-out,* and *practice*. With someone who works in finance, there are many words one can use to connect in a way that has meaning, words such as *investment, assets,* and *futures*.

Joining clients is an important part of both the initial phase and the treatment phase with those who suffer from meaninglessness. This approach requires that the counselor meet the client as an authentic, vulnerable human being. The ministry of Jesus was marked by the traits of authenticity and vulnerability. It was also characterized by the way he connected with individuals. He had a way of seeing persons in a crowd and joining them, as Zaccheus found when he looked down from a sycamore tree into the eyes of one looking up at him. And those who encountered his gaze and felt his presence, changed their ways and sensed a new meaning in their lives.

CHAPTER THIRTY-SIX

THE WIND FROM HEAVEN

THE FIRST CHAPTER of this book referred to Solomon's metaphor for meaninglessness—"chasing the wind." I believe if we go to the center of a problem ourselves, or with a client, we will find the solution there. Jesus went to the center of the sin problem—the cross—because he knew that's where the solution was. And if we go to the center of the problem of chasing the wind, face the meaninglessness squarely, and surrender to God, we will discover another wind, one which does not empty our life, but rather fills it. Luke describes the coming of the Holy Spirit at Pentecost, "Suddenly a sound like the blowing of a violent wind came from heaven and filled the whole house where they were sitting" (Acts 2:2 NIV).

217

From that point on the disciples were impelled by the Holy Spirit. Their lives were still difficult but now they had direction and power. Living a meaningless life—chasing the wind—is terribly hard work, but the message of the Bible is that being led by the Spirit of God is not easy either. I grew up a Kansas farm boy, feeling the strong winds. They blow in Nebraska, too, and now when I feel or hear them, I often think of the Holy Spirit and realize that just as the wind has never been tamed, so the Spirit of God is not tame.

Life in the Spirit

The spiritual life is, of course, the remedy for the meaningless life. And the Holy Spirit's presence is a constant reminder of Jesus Christ and his love. It is the Holy Spirit who releases our clients to become all that God made them able to become, to move through their suffering to find a new purpose in life.

Life in the Spirit enables our clients, as well as ourselves, to dereflect from a continual focus on "me" and my happiness. I like the metaphor of the eye that Frankl uses for this kind of dereflection. He says that the ability of the eye to see its world is based on its inability to see itself. If it does see itself, its vision is impaired. If it sees its cataract, vision is impaired by cloudiness; if it sees its glaucoma, its vision is impaired by a halo. But the healthy eye, just as the healthy person, overlooks itself and is fully available for use.[1]

Solomon, as he wrote Ecclesiastes, was a clear example of hyperreflection. He sat and reflected and brooded about meaninglessness and chasing the wind until he was of little use to anyone. But he observed and recorded an amazing example of dereflection. He noticed that when one accepts and enjoys his work and his lot in life, "this is a gift of God. He seldom reflects on the days of his life, because God keeps him occupied with gladness of heart" (Eccles. 5:19–20 NIV). Those who can do this are useful to others because, like the healthy eye, they are reflecting not on themselves but on the world around them.

Spiritual Hunger

One of the great "finds" of my life was a set of *The Harvard Classics*, for twenty-five cents apiece, in a Goodwill store.

I have been rereading Pascal lately from that series. His *Thoughts, Letters, and Minor Works* make up one volume in the set.[2] He made a comment on the need for spiritual hunger that I have been considering: "We do not weary of eating and sleeping every day, for hunger and sleepiness recur. Without that we should weary of them. So, without the hunger for spiritual things, we weary of them."[3]

It occurred to me in my first reading of Pascal's insight that we would do well to arouse spiritual hunger in our clients (as well as in ourselves). But, as I thought longer about this, it seemed to me that hunger is a natural state that, in a healthy person, does not need to be aroused. Perhaps that's it. As we focus more and more on ourselves (hyperreflect), we become spiritually unhealthy and lose our spiritual hunger. Perhaps the physical mirror of this is one who has the disease anorexia nervosa and, although emaciated, has no appetite. She is so hyperreflected on herself that she actually resists hunger pangs.

So what does a counselor do with one who has an eating disorder? We help the person dereflect and begin to see the real world. This same approach can be useful in helping ourselves or our clients when there is little or no spiritual hunger. We help them dereflect, and then help them see their spiritual world as it is. This may be done through Socratic questioning and through discussing and experiencing the love of God. Perhaps most of all, we stir the spiritual hunger of our clients by serving as spiritual reminders ourselves. As Henri Nouwen said, "Once we have heard, seen, watched, and touched the Word, who is life, we cannot do other than be living reminders."[4]

This "living reminder" idea of the counselor returns us to the importance of "presence" in counseling. I know that I have been helped simply by the presence of others, and some have said they have been helped by my presence. An important, healing part of what suffering clients experience in our presence is love.

THE SPIRIT, LOVE, AND MEANING

Love, of course, is the gift of the Holy Spirit. And it is love that allows us to understand our clients as they are and as they can be. Clients who are struggling with meaninglessness need help in both these areas. They usually do not see themselves nor the world realistically, nor do they have any hope that things can be different. Our love for clients allows them to hear our challenge of their distorted view of their world, and then to gain courage to begin responding to what God is asking of them. Their mission from God will come through the Holy Spirit. Jesus said to his disciples, "You must wait in the city until the power from above comes down upon you" (Luke 24:49 TEV). The power and direction of the Holy Spirit can bring new meaning and zest to the client.

PART FOUR

PREVENTING MEANINGLESSNESS

THE PROBLEM OF meaninglessness is one that lends itself to prevention. And prevention is of great importance. By expending creative thought and effort here, we can keep considerable human suffering from occurring, and we can help people enhance their productiveness.

There are many actions that local churches can take that will give its members and friends opportunities to discover meaningful tasks and relationships. Professionals who view themselves not only as counselors, but also as change agents, can use what they have learned clinically about the causes of futility to create new paths to meaning in churches, families, and the workplace. Some directions these paths might take are described in this section.

CHAPTER THIRTY-SEVEN

MEANING, JUSTICE, AND SERVICE

MOST OF THIS BOOK has focused on ways of responding to those who are suffering from a crisis of meaninglessness. But this is not the only crisis facing our world. In his book *The Apostolic Imperative*, Carl Braaten calls Christians to the awareness that there are "two major crises that threaten the life and well-being of millions, even billions, of people today. The first is the existential crisis of meaning, and the second is the global crisis of misery."[1] The crisis of meaning confronts the world of affluent people. The crisis of misery gnaws at the world of the poverty stricken.

Although the search for meaning is very important in life, it is not to be placed above all other values. William Pannell has spoken persuasively on this point. He has said that evangelical Christians "refuse to challenge the fundamental assumptions of a culture where the pursuit of individual meaning is more valued than justice."[2] He has noted that this is part of the larger American societal concern that prioritizes meaning above ethics and morality, and has done so for years.[3]

The biblical call, both Old Testament and New Testament, for justice is strong and clear. That call is echoed silently by the needs of the voiceless in every community—the poor, the minorities, and the emotionally ill. When Jesus read from the scroll of Isaiah at Nazareth, he read about his anointing to preach good news to the poor *and* to relieve human suffering.

Is there a *common* solution to the gigantic twin crisis of meaninglessness and misery that Braaten described? One such solution is service. In an act of service we can prevent or reduce the misery of another and discover meaning for ourselves. Meaning comes not through an insight, but a response—an action. This response needs to be an unselfish one. We cannot seek meaning and find it any more than we can gain happiness by seeking it. Meaning comes to us as the by-product of responding to a cause or to another's needs. It is this attitude of responsiveness that connects the two great crises of meaning and justice. We see in the model of Jesus how an attitude determines a response: "Your attitude should be the same as that of Christ Jesus" (Phil. 2:5) who took "the very nature of a servant" (Phil. 2:7). He "did not come to be served, but to serve" (Mark 10:45 all NIV).

SERVICE AS A WAY TO PREVENT MEANINGLESSNESS

A twenty-year-old woman put it this way:

I wonder why God put me on the earth? What is my main purpose? Is there something I am supposed to do to help others? There must be something special out there waiting for me, but what?

We seem to have as "original equipment" the belief that we should serve God and our fellow human beings. Counselors can use this "pull" to help clients achieve meaning.

Self-transcendence is the fulfillment of meaning by giving ourselves to a person or a cause greater than ourselves. Pastors and other Christian counselors can also act as change agents to direct people into meaningful service and thus prevent the existential vacuum of meaninglessness. The first task in moving people toward service is motivation.

Motivation to Serve

The success of volunteerism in America is sufficient evidence that service does not have to be paid for in order to get people to do it. But it does need to be significant and of value to those served. As the college student asked above, "Is there something I'm supposed to do to *help others*?" That is where the meaning is.

The next factor in motivation is to help match people's mission with the needs that exist. This need to match is often overlooked in church recruitment of volunteers, and members feel pressured to take a position such as a church school teacher or an usher when their gifts and calling lie elsewhere. The matching process requires a great deal of listening, discernment regarding spiritual gifts, and some questioning to draw out interests and mission. One may not be inclined to lead junior church but get very excited about writing a computer software program to assist the church's financial planners.

Response to Needs

In a city church in the midwest, one of the adult church school classes was decimated by divorce. Some of the remaining couples got together to talk about a response that could help others in the church. Since that time this small group of couples has sought training in counseling and intervention skills and have made themselves available to other couples and individuals who are hurting because of marriage difficulties. This example, along with many others, suggests that the pastor and church boards do not have to announce all the tasks to be done in a church. They need to support those who see the need and respond to tasks. Roger Fredrikson's book, *God Loves the Dandelions,* describes a church that took this approach.[4]

There are many people sitting in worship services each week

who look like they are making it in life but they are "putting on a happy face" to cover the emptiness they feel every day because they are frantically "chasing the wind" of a life that is no longer full of meaning. They will need a spiritual renewal to get turned around. In addition, they will need a place to serve.

The Team Concept

Many places of service in church are "Lone Ranger" positions. The advantage of team service is that the talking and listening and joint service build a cohesive group and offer the special meaning of a shared adventure. Pastors and lay persons alike can help small groups focus their concerns. Then the group can be helped to make the transition from an interest group to a mission group, as the small group did from the church school class, above, in an effort to help hurting couples.

The Prevention of Meaninglessness—A Matter of Action

We discover our own meaning in life as we *act* on our answer to the question, "What does God require of me?" This means that churches and other Christian groups need to listen very carefully to their members, and respond in ways that will help them find their unique mission. However, this interchange is not enough. The meaning comes not with the insight but the action. We will not have prevented meaninglessness until we help people respond.

The Counselor as Change Agent

Christian counselors are in an excellent position to act as change agents. We can make a difference in the structures of the organizations we are in, so that there are more avenues of genuine service.

CHAPTER THIRTY-EIGHT

MEANING AND HEALTH

Sir William Osler, a major contributor to modern medicine, gave this advice to his medical students, "Ask not what kind of disease the person has, ask what kind of person has the disease."[1] This statement implies that there are personality and behavioral factors, in addition to the recognized organic factors, that contribute to or are a part of the disease.

As counselors, we cannot be moral and ethical and yet overlook the health condition of our clients. Good health can contribute to a meaningful life, but the reverse is also true. The evidences are coming in now on many of the behavioral and environmental conditions that impact on health. Carl Thoresen and Jean Eagleston of Stanford University have reported on some of the most striking evidences in a major article, "Counseling for Health," in *The Counseling Psychologist.*[2]

SEVEN HEALTH PRACTICES

One study examined the health practices of nearly seven thousand California adults for over five years, and then did a follow-up with five thousand of these adults four years later. The seven behaviors studied were:

ate breakfast almost every day
rarely or never ate between meals
slept seven to eight hours daily
maintained normal weight adjusted for height, age, and sex
never smoked cigarettes
avoided alcohol or used alcohol moderately
had regular physical activity.[3]

The findings of the follow-up study confirmed those of the five-year program. Those men who practiced all seven of the above behaviors had a mortality rate about four times lower than those who practiced none or only a few of the behaviors. The comparable mortality rate for women was two times lower.[4]

SOCIAL NETWORK FACTORS

The same five thousand people were also studied over the nine-and-a-half-year period as to four variables of social network: marital status, number of contacts with close friends and relatives, frequency of those contacts, and membership in churches and other groups. The findings? "The age-adjusted risk of death for males with the fewest social contacts was found to be 2.3 times greater than those with the most social contacts; for females the rate was 2.8 to 1."[5] Friendships may be a key component in longevity of life.

INTERNAL STRESS FACTORS

The Type A Behavior Pattern (TABP) is a well-known chronic stress approach to life. This style of life includes a hard-driving competitiveness, feeling time-pressured, and an easily aroused anger and hostility. Using standard psychological and physical tests, researchers have discovered a significant positive relationship between the TABP and the amount of coronary artery obstruction.[6] One study of over two hundred and fifty physicians found that those above the median in hostility were six times more likely to die earlier than expected, as compared to those who scored low on hostility. Thoresen and Eagleston caution that the above factors, as is the case with most statistical studies, cannot be considered *causative* factors. Yet, the evidences are thought-provoking.

IMPLICATIONS OF THIS HEALTH
RESEARCH FOR THE COUNSELOR

So what difference does this all make for the counselor concerned with meaning? One implication is that the counselor may wish to take a personal inventory. Values, of course, are caught, not taught. The counselor often says more as a model than through words. This includes the seven health factors, level of social network support, and TABP. Positive changes in these areas in our own lives may point the way to health for our counselees as well as be life-lengthening for us. The level of social network support ties in with the logotherapy concept of self-transcendence. If we are invested in another person, if we are living beyond ourselves, that person then increases our social network contacts.

THE URGENT AND THE IMPORTANT

Concerning TABP, there is a common theme among those who display this pattern—"drivenness." Speed has taken priority over direction. We have succumbed to the hazard that Charles Hummel has warned about, "Your greatest danger is letting the urgent things crowd out the important."[7] The counselor who works from the viewpoint of meaning has much to offer those clients afflicted by TABP. Through Socratic questioning we may be able to help them slow down a little and attempt to discover what life is asking of them. One question could be, "If you go on living like you are, what will be the condition of your health ten years from now?" Another question asked by logotherapists is, "As you visualize yourself on the last day of your life looking back over your life, what would you have needed to have done or been in order to feel fulfilled?" Still another question could be, "Is there a way to change your lifestyle so you can enjoy and be more physically active with your grandchildren (or nieces, nephews, and so forth) as they grow up?" And, finally, "How satisfied are you with the way you have been caring for the gift of your body with which God has entrusted you?" The body may not be as important as the mind or the spirit, but it is worth the counselor's careful consideration.

RELAXATION

We need to help the client continue to have relaxed times. The word "hypertension" speaks eloquently of the need for relaxation. Yet we have to work at relaxing. Why? Perhaps because we fear a lack of control. The word "lax" is paired with other words, such as "lax morals," and "lax bowels" (hence "laxative"). It is not good to be out of control in those areas! So when we try to "re-lax," to become lax again, we don't like the out-of-control feeling. When we are relaxed, there is a sense in which we are out of control. We cannot jump into action immediately.

I have become convinced that we need to help some clients deal with the issue of control before they can relax. The control issue has to do not only with our bodies, but with all of life. We have to be willing to be out of control in some areas of our lives. What about our relationship with God? Surrender is a more apt word than control. And creativity? We are in control when we reason, but not when we create. We don't know how that poem, painting, or child will "turn out." And our friendships? We don't control them unless they are dominant-submissive relationships.

Relaxation is necessary for good health, effective learning, and friendly relationships. We will be useful to our clients if we help them find a way to relinquish control and relax. A Socratic dialogue on the felt need to control can be a beginning.

OUR HEALTH ACCOUNT

Logotherapists sometimes use the phrase "overdrawing your health account." Contrary to overdrawing our bank account, it is a good thing to overdraw our health account. This phrase emphasizes that if our lives have meaning, our bodies are thereby "inspired" to do better than they normally would. I had a friend who lived to be ninety-six. She had polio at eleven, and was confined to a wheelchair for eighty-five years. She had several operations in the later part of her life. None seemed to slow her down. Her skin felt young to the touch. She was one of a number of people whom I have studied who are in their nineties.

One aspect of the study was interviewing her relatives about her, and another was a taped interview with her. Several key elements emerged from these interviews: 1) She never complained; 2) she had many friends; 3) she was always busy either sewing (her trade by which she supported herself all her life) or helping others; 4) she gave many gifts to others, often items that she sewed; 5) she had a strong faith in Christ, and lived it. She is the best example I know of someone who "overdrew her health account."

Lawrence LeShan, one who has spent most of his career working with advanced cancer patients, makes a strong case for the connection between meaning and health.[8] He suggests that we ask ourselves such questions as whether or not we have many interests rather than only one, and whether we are doing what we want to with our lives. The woman above was one who could have answered "yes" to these questions. LeShan's last question is important to answer "no" to: "If I were told I had a terminal illness, would I experience some sense of relief?"[9] A "yes" answer here would indicate that we had stopped responding to life, that it no longer had meaning.

CHAPTER THIRTY-NINE

TRAINING LISTENER-RESPONDERS IN CHURCHES

MORTON KELSEY HAS given the church a dynamic challenge: "I wonder if a Christian parish church is offering genuine Christian education if it does not provide training in listening skills and offer listening classes for children and adults."[1]

I've been involved in leading seminars in local churches for the last fifteen years to train participants in listening responding skills. The methods for lay-counseling training have been developed to the point where it can be quite effective. What is needed, besides the participants, is first a skilled counselor-teacher who can *demonstrate* these skills, and then assist the participants as they *practice* the skills. Counseling is a skill as well as an art, so supervised practice is a necessity.

The counselor-teacher does not necessarily need to hold those professional titles. Rather, that person needs to be able to do those functions. The second component is a curriculum to follow. Gary Collins, in the first book in this RCC series, lists "Selected Helpful Books and Training Programs for Lay Counselor Training."[2] My book on this subject, *Connecting with a Friend,* comes with a "Built-in Workbook" for learning eighteen counseling skills.[3] The skill training offered in that book has been field-tested with over a thousand lay counselors in college residence halls, retirement centers, nursing homes, and churches, as well as with several hundred lay counselors taking a college course.

Gathering the People for the Training

The participants I have trained in churches have included church board members, groups specifically selected because of proven gifts in helping, church school classes, and church paraprofessional staffs. I recommend the use of an existing "vehicle" in the church so that no more time is taken from already busy people. A church school class can accomplish a great deal in a thirteen-week quarter. A diaconate or other church board can use the first thirty minutes of its meeting for this training.

INCLUDING THE MEANING DIMENSION

Any good training in counseling skills will help participants improve their ability to counsel for meaning. Effective listeners learn to "follow" people to the center of their concerns. That is where the meaning is. But, as one person asked, "What do I do then?" This is the place to put Socratic questioning skills into practice. I have found it helpful to use non-religious questions in an attempt to get at meaning. One such learning experience I have modified from a question asked by Mignon Eisenberg.[4]

I ask people in a group setting, "Suppose all the people you love—family and friends—are in this room. They have been asked by a producer to make a movie of your life from birth to now. Zap! They have done it. There is only one task that remains before the film is distributed. You are to entitle it. Give it a title that will fit on a marquee—no more than four or five words." After they have done this, arrange for small group sharing of titles and discussion of them.

The second half of the experience follows: "The movie was a box office success. The producer returns to give you a contract for a sequel. This second movie will begin at this moment and continue until your death. You will help write the script, act in it, and be co-director. Now imagine that the movie is finished. What will you entitle *this* film?" Obviously, this second half of the experience has a great deal to do with meaning. Small group and total group discussion of titles will help the "main characters" learn a great deal about how they view their mission in life. The experience also gives the participants a sense of time. We have no control over the first film. But the sequel is a reminder that we have a "second chance" now to carry out our mission in life.

THE CONTRIBUTIONS OF SMALL GROUPS TO MEANING

Meaning often comes to us through listening and responding in small groups such as the ones mentioned above because such groups recapitulate our growing-up family. Arthur Jersild commented on this connection when he observed that most of our attitudes about ourselves come from an interpersonal setting (the family) and, therefore, "it is likely that only in an interpersonal setting can a person be helped to come to grips with some of the meanings of these attitudes."[5]

My own estimate of the value of small groups for meaning in life has not dimmed, in spite of intensive study and leading over two-hundred personal growth or encounter groups. Each time I start with a new group I feel like a novice. It takes a while to get over this initial crisis in my confidence level. Perhaps it is right that we should feel like novices with any new group no matter how experienced we are, because we have no experience with *this* group. Each group has a life and personality all its own; we can control the development of a group about as easily as we can steer a cloud. There are many kinds of groups that offer the potential of increasing our meaning in life.

Renewal-Support-Training Groups

For the last six years I have been a member of a small caring group with two of my closest friends. The renewal component is provided when one of us feels discouraged or burned out. The support comes each week or every other week as we talk together. And the training element is the Bible study that we usually have going together. I have noticed how support groups come and go. Those that have the training component—usually Bible study—seem to have longer lives.

An executive came to me for counseling about a year ago and said that life did not have the meaning for him that it used to. He thought he was "falling apart" and probably should set up a series of individual counseling sessions. He was effective in his work. He had an excellent marriage and a fine family. He was a committed Christian. After listening for an hour or so, I recommended that, instead of beginning personal counseling, he form the kind of group I have discussed here. It appeared to me that he had no close friends other than his wife. He needed a "soul-friend" or two, with whom he could share intimately. I suggested the following criterion for forming a group with one or two others: "Are these persons ones with whom I have a spiritual kinship or ones with whom I think I could have a spiritual kinship?" It is this quality in a group that provides the basis for meaning to emerge. Since our talk, he has formed such a group with two other men and they meet regularly for fellowship, prayer, and study. He says this on-going experience is adding a new dimension of meaning to his life.

Paul Ford has described soul friendship as characterized by two characteristics: they hold the other accountable in their Christian life, and they encourage each other.[6] A soul friend thus helps us avoid both self-deception and discouragement in our spiritual life and battles.

Small Groups in the Church

In addition to serving some of the purposes of the renewal-support group discussed above, small groups which are composed of members of a church offer an additional advantage—a sense of spiritual family. The group is not "free-standing," for it belongs to this particular family of God. This awareness brings a special relational quality to the group. Faith at Work, with its strong commitment to relational Christianity, has contributed immeasurably to the number and quality of small fellowship groups. They have excellent strategies and resources available for the formation and nourishing of small groups.[7]

CONTINUING YOUR LEARNING

I hope this book is useful to you as you work to make your counseling skills even more effective. If you choose to continue learning in this area of counseling and the search for meaning, you will find the annotated bibliography helpful. It appears in the Appendix. In addition, some of the references in the Notes will direct you to significant resources. If you desire information regarding formal training in logotherapy, the Institute of Logotherapy can provide that.[8] Also, you may find the Self-Directed Learning Project idea useful. Establish your specific objectives for learning, then design strategies and resources for achieving those objectives.

Best wishes to you in your learning and growth.

APPENDIX

Useful Resources on Counseling for Meaning

Bolles, Richard N., *The Three Boxes of Life: And How to Get Out of Them* (Berkeley: Ten Speed Press, 1978, 1981). This is an extraordinary book about learning, working, and playing. It is also a book about discovering meaning in life. The emphasis throughout the book is on finding our mission in work and life and becoming effective in carrying it out.

Crumbaugh, James C., *Everything to Gain: A Guide to Self-fulfillment through Logoanalysis* (Chicago: Nelson-Hall Co., 1973). Logoanalysis is a systematic approach to finding ourselves and a purpose in life. Crumbaugh has based his logoanalysis approach squarely on logotherapy. There are many exercises and guided experiences in the book.

°Fabry, Joseph B., *The Pursuit of Meaning* (New York: Harper & Row, 1968, 1980). Dr. Fabry is one of the foremost interpreters of Frankl and logotherapy. Fabry's positions as the editor of *The International Forum for Logotherapy* and as a long-time executive director of the Institute of Logotherapy in Berkeley have kept him in close touch with Frankl and with the movement and literature of logotherapy. His book includes discussions of values, conscience, freedom, responsibility, and the reality of religion. He also has a chapter on the application of logotherapy.

237

°Fabry, Joseph B., Reuven P. Bulka, and William S. Sahakian (eds.), *Logotherapy in Action* (New York: Jason Aronson, 1979). This book places logotherapy in perspective psychologically, describes logo-therapy's techniques, its medical uses, and applications to youth, the addicted, and the broader concerns of communities.

Frankl, Viktor E., *The Doctor and the Soul* (New York: Vintage Books, 1955, 1973). This was originally published in 1946 as *Arztliche Seelsorge*. Frankl describes existential analysis as this method of therapy relates to the meaning of life and death, to suffering (including his own in the concentration camp), to work, and to love. He also discusses anxiety neurosis, obsessional neurosis, melancholia, and schizophrenia.

Frankl, Viktor E., *Man's Search for Meaning* (New York: Pocket Books, 1939, 1963). The original English title was *From Death-Camp to Existentialism*. This book is divided into two sections: The first two-thirds is a gripping account of his experiences in the concentration camps. The last third describes the basic concepts of logotherapy.

Frankl, Viktor E., *The Unconscious God* (New York: Simon and Schuster, 1948, 1975). The original title was *Dor Unbewusste Gott*. Frankl's thesis here is that in every person's unconscious depths there is a deeply rooted religious sense. The book hinges on the concept of conscience. In fact, his last chapter (nearly half the book) gives his revised views on conscience after twenty-five years of further thought and research.

Frankl, Viktor E., *The Unheard Cry for Meaning* (New York: A Touchstone Book, Simon and Schuster, 1978). Frankl discusses the evidences for the silent thirst for meaning, and relates this quest to humanism, sex, temporality, sports, and the application of paradoxical intention and dereflection. His treatment of "Sports—The Asceticism of Today" is a fresh view of modern athletics.

The International Forum for Logotherapy. This journal on the search for meaning is an excellent resource for discovering current issues, applications, and research findings in logotherapy. It has been published twice yearly since 1978. Most former issues may be purchased from the Institute of Logotherapy at the address noted at the end of this appendix.

Kelsey, Morton T., *Caring* (New York: Paulist Press, 1981). Kelsey deals head-on with the reality and difficulty of love. He also deals in a useful way with the presence of evil in ourselves and in others. It is an excellent resource on discovering meaning in life by practicing relational Christianity.

LeShan, Lawrence, *You Can Fight for Your Life* (New York: M. Evans and Co., 1980). LeShan has spent most of his career as a psychologist working with advanced cancer patients in New York City. This is the story of how many of these patients achieved long-term remission after they were helped to "find their song and sing it," to discover what life was asking of them.

Leslie, Robert C., *Jesus as Counselor* (Nashville: Abingdon, 1965, 1982). This is a case study approach—such as Zacchaeus, Simon the Pharisee, and Mary and Martha—to the ministry of Jesus. He shows how Jesus worked to bring new meaning to lives, to realize creative and experiential values, to realize attitudinal values, and to restore human dignity. Leslie's views reflect his study with Frankl.

*Lukas, Elisabeth, *Meaningful Living* (Berkeley: An Institute of Logotherapy Press Book, published by Grove Press, Inc., New York, 1984, 1986). Lukas did her Ph.D. work under the supervision of Frankl. In the preface of this book, Frankl relates what he told Lukas after hearing her lecture, "Somehow it is easier to know I'll die—being assured that my legacy rests in your hands." Lukas describes the basic steps and methods of logotherapy, and provides thirty-six case studies to illustrate their application.

*Lukas, Elisabeth, *Meaning in Suffering* (Berkeley: Institute of Logotherapy Press, 1986). People come for counseling because they are suffering. Lukas describes her logotherapeutic approach to reduce human suffering, with illustrations from twenty-five case studies. She deals with comfort, guilt, resistance, joy, and responsibility as these relate to the question of meaning.

May, Rollo, *The Discovery of Being* (New York: W. W. Norton & Co., Inc., 1983). This is a good reference on existential psychology and its contributions to therapy. The reader is helped to see the importance of focusing on the client rather than on a method.

Miller, Calvin, *A Hunger for Meaning* (Downers Grove, IL: InterVarsity Press, 1984). This is a useful new edition of Miller's 1973 book, *A Thirst for Meaning*. He discusses such topics as reason and faith, the absurd, evil, materialism, and "Christ the Healer."

Nouwen, Henri J. M., *The Living Reminder* (New York: Seabury Press, 1981). This brief book provides many insights into the resources of those who would minister. His treatment of memory and "reminders" is simple, personal, and remarkable.

Patterson, C. H., *Theories of Counseling and Psychotherapy*, 4th ed., (New York: Harper & Row, 1986). This is one of the most accurate and thorough comparisons of the major approaches to counseling.

Patterson summarizes the theories of seventeen theorists and practitioners, including Frankl.

Tournier, Paul, *The Meaning of Gifts* (Richmond, VA: John Knox Press, 1963). Tournier tells in this little book what he has learned from his clients about the meaning of gifts. He deals especially with parents' gifts to their children.

Tournier, Paul, *The Meaning of Persons* (New York: Harper & Bros., 1957). Tournier gives a biblical perspective of the subject. He also supports his views with other literature and with references to patients. It is an existential book emphasizing the need to choose.

*These books are distributed by the Institute of Logotherapy, Administrative Office, P. O. Box 2852, Saratoga, CA 95070.

NOTES

Introduction

1. Malcolm S. Knowles, *The Modern Practice of Adult Education* (Chicago: Follett Publishing Co., 1980). Knowles's earlier book, *Self-Directed Learning* (Chicago: Follett Publishing Co., 1975) is a more concise statement of this educational method.

Chapter 1. Chasing the Wind

1. Mignon Eisenberg, "Logotherapy—Prescription for Survival," *The International Forum for Logotherapy*, Vol. 5, No. 2 (Fall/Winter 1982), 68.
2. Rollo May, *Man's Search for Himself* (New York: W. W. Norton & Co., Inc., 1953), 14.

Chapter 2. The Nature of Meaninglessness

1. Sidney M. Jourard, *Disclosing Man to Himself* (New York: D. Van Nostrand Co., 1968), 116.
2. Ibid., 117.
3. Viktor Frankl, *Man's Search for Meaning* (New York: Pocket Books, 1963), 169.

4. Elisabeth Lukas, "Logotherapy's Message to Parents and Teachers," *The International Forum for Logotherapy*, Vol. 1, No. 1 (Winter 1978-Spring 1979), 10.

5. Viktor Frankl, *The Unconscious God* (New York: Simon and Schuster, 1975), 96.

6. Brana Lobel and Robert Hirschfeld, booklet entitled "Depression: What We Know," U. S. Department of Health and Human Services, Public Health Service, Alcohol, Drug Abuse, and Mental Health Administration, DHHS Pub. # (ADM) 84–1318 (Washington, D.C.: U. S. Government Printing Office, 1984), 3.

7. Ibid.

8. Roberta Caplan, "Alcoholism," *Academic American Encyclopedia* (Danbury, Conn.: Grolier, Inc., 1985), 265.

9. *ADAMHA Data Book*, U. S. Department of Health and Human Services, Public Health Service, Alcohol, Drug Abuse, and Mental Health Administration, DHHS Pub. # (ADM) 84–662 (Washington, D.C.: U. S. Government Printing Office, 1983), 14.

10. Ibid., 15.

11. Uniform Crime Reports for the United States, "Crime in the United States, 1985," Federal Bureau of Investigation, U. S. Department of Justice (Washington, D.C.: U. S. Government Printing Office, 1985).

12. Steven R. Schlesinger, "Households Touched by Crime, 1985," U. S. Department of Justice, Bureau of Statistics (Washington, D.C.: U. S. Government Printing Office, Bulletin, June 1986), 1.

13. "Violent Crime in the United States," U. S. Department of Justice, Bureau of Justice and Statistics, National Indicators System (Washington, D.C.: U. S. Government Printing Office, 1982), 21.

14. James A. Weed, "Suicide in the United States," Ch. 6 in Carl A. Taube and Sally A. Barrett (eds.), *Mental Health, United States, 1985*, U. S. Department of Health and Human Services, DHHS Pub. # (ADM) 85–1378 (Washington, D.C.: U. S. Government Printing Office, 1985), 135.

15. Frederick K. Goodwin, "Medicine for the Layman: Depressive and Manic Depressive Illness," U. S. Department of Health and Human Services, NIH Pub. # 82–1940 (Washington, D.C.: U. S. Government Printing Service, 1982), 13.

16. Ibid.

17. Paul Tillich, *The Courage to Be* (New Haven: Yale University Press, 1952), 173.

18. Robert N. Bellah, et al, *Habits of the Heart* (Berkeley: Regents of the University of California, 1985), 282.

19. Ibid., 282.

20. Viktor Frankl, *The Unheard Cry for Meaning* (New York: A Touchstone Book, Simon and Schuster, 1978), 17.

21. Ibid., 95–96.

22. Marv Miller, "A Detailed Factsheet on Suicide" (The Information Center, 6377 Lake Apopka Place, San Diego, CA 92119, 1984), 1–14.

Chapter 3. The Causes and Dynamics of Meaninglessness

1. Kenneth C. Green and Alexander W. Astin, "The Mood on Campus: More Conservative or Just More Materialistic?" *Educational Record*, Vol. 67, No. 1 (Winter 1985), 48.

2. Joseph B. Fabry, *The Pursuit of Meaning* (New York: Harper and Row, 1980), 92.

3. Karl Menninger, *Whatever Became of Sin?* (New York: Hawthorn, 1973).

4. M. Scott Peck, *People of the Lie* (New York: Simon and Schuster, 1983), 127.

5. Paul Tournier, *The Meaning of Gifts* (Richmond: John Knox Press, 1963), 31.

6. Ibid.

7. Frankl, *Man's Search for Meaning*, 157.

8. Ibid.

9. Ibid.

10. Ibid., 169.

11. Ibid., 173.

12. Elisabeth Lukas, *Meaningful Living* (Berkeley: Institute of Logotherapy Press, 1984), 24.

13. Frankl, *Man's Search for Meaning*, 163.

14. Ibid.

Part II. Specific Counseling Approaches and Methods

1. Knowles, *The Modern Practice of Adult Education*, 53–54.

Chapter 4. Love and Meaning

1. May, *Man's Search for Himself*, 241.
2. M. Scott Peck, *The Road Less Traveled* (New York: A Touchstone Book, Simon and Schuster, 1978), 82.
3. Morton T. Kelsey, *Caring* (New York: Paulist Press, 1981), 101.
4. Henri J. M. Nouwen, *The Living Reminder* (New York: Seabury Press, 1981), 31.
5. Ibid.
6. Henry Drummond, *The Greatest Thing in the World* (New York: Greystone Press, 1951).
7. Ibid., 102.
8. Ibid., 103–4.

Chapter 5. Counseling as Releasing

1. Rollo May, *The Discovery of Being* (New York: W. W. Norton & Co., 1983), 9.
2. Frankl, *Man's Search for Meaning*, 174.
3. Paul Tournier, *The Meaning of Persons* (New York: Harper & Bros., 1957).
4. Ibid., 32.
5. Blaise Pascal, *Thoughts, Letters, and Minor Works, The Harvard Classics*, ed. by Charles W. Elliot (New York: P. F. Collier & Son, 1910), 157.

Chapter 6. The Existential Approach to Counseling

1. Paul Welter, *Connecting with a Friend* (Wheaton, Ill.: Tyndale House Publishers, Inc., 1985), 74.
2. Ibid., 73.
3. Herbert Benson, *The Relaxation Response* (New York: William Morrow, 1975), and *Beyond the Relaxation Response* (New York: Berkeley Books, 1984). Readers desiring further information about the therapists noted in figure 2 may find it in C. H. Patterson, *Theories of Counseling and Psychotherapy* (New York: Harper & Row, 1986), and William A. Wallace, *Theories of Counseling and Psychotherapy* (Boston: Allyn and Bacon, 1986). Dolores Krieger's "Therapeutic Touch" is discussed in Catherine C. Brown (ed.), *The*

Many Facets of Touch (Skillman, N.J.: Johnson & Johnson Baby Products Co., 1984).

4. F. S. Perls, *Gestalt Therapy Verbatim* and *In and Out of the Garbage Pail.* Both are 1969 books published by Real People Press, Lafayette, Calif. Perls was trained in psychoanalysis. He saw Gestalt Therapy as one of the existential therapies. Gestalt Therapy would also fit under the "Senses" heading in figure 2 because of Perls's much-quoted line, "Lose your mind and come to your senses."

5. Frank B. Minirth and Paul D. Meier, *Happiness Is a Choice* (Grand Rapids, Mich.: Baker Book House, 1978).

6. Irvin D. Yalom, *Existential Psychotherapy* (New York: Basic Books, Inc., 1980).

7. Ibid., 8.

8. Ibid., 483.

9. Ibid.

10. Ibid., 481.

11. Ibid., 482.

12. Ibid., 422.

13. Fabry, *The Pursuit of Meaning,* 136.

Chapter 7. The Contributions of Viktor Frankl

1. Fabry, *The Pursuit of Meaning,* 9.

2. Ibid., 8.

3. Frankl, *Man's Search for Meaning,* 122.

4. Ibid., 126.

5. Viktor Frankl, *The Doctor and the Soul* (New York: Vintage Books, 1973).

6. Frankl, *The Unheard Cry for Meaning,* 20.

7. Frankl, *The Doctor and the Soul,* xxi.

8. Yalom, *Existential Psychotherapy,* 479.

9. Frankl, *Man's Search for Meaning,* 154.

10. Ibid.

11. Frankl, *The Doctor and the Soul,* 8.

12. From Frankl, *Logos und existenz,* 51, quoted by Donald F. Tweedie, Jr., in *Logotherapy and the Christian Faith* (Grand Rapids, Mich.: Baker Book House, 1961), 69.

13. Frankl, *The Unheard Cry for Meaning,* 47–48.

14. Ibid., 48.

15. Frankl, *The Doctor and the Soul,* 5.

16. Adrian van Kaam, "Foundation Formation and the Will to

Meaning," *The International Forum for Logotherapy*, No. 3 (Spring 1980), 59.

17. Tweedie, *Logotherapy and the Christian Faith*, 179.

18. Fabry, *The Pursuit of Meaning*, 155.

19. Yalom, *Existential Psychotherapy*, 442.

20. Ibid., 423.

21. Ibid.

22. Ibid.

23. Robert C. Leslie, *Jesus as Counselor* (Nashville: Abingdon, 1982).

24. Ibid., preface.

Chapter 8. The Logotherapy Approach

1. Elisabeth Lukas, *Meaning in Suffering* (Berkeley: Institute of Logotherapy Press, 1986).

2. Ibid., 99–100.

3. William Glasser, *Reality Therapy* (New York: Harper & Row, 1975), 35–41.

4. Ibid., 37.

5. Fabry, *The Pursuit of Meaning*, 132.

6. Lukas, *Meaningful Living*, 46.

7. Ibid.

8. Frankl, *The Unheard Cry for Meaning*, 35.

9. Ibid.

10. Bruce Larson, *There's a Lot More to Health Than Not Being Sick* (Waco, Tex.: Word Books, 1981).

11. Raymond E. Vath, *Counseling Those with Eating Disorders*, Resources for Christian Counseling, Vol. 4 (Waco, Tex.: Word Books, 1986).

12. Lukas, *Meaning in Suffering*, 57.

13. Ibid.

14. The Institute of Logotherapy, P. O. Box 156, Berkeley, CA 94704, is the address for information on training, education, research, and for editorial matters, such as submission of manuscripts for the Institute Press and for *The International Forum for Logotherapy*. It exists to teach and expand logotherapy throughout the world. The Institute of Logotherapy, Administrative Office, P. O. Box 2852, Saratoga, CA 95070, is the address for general information, membership, subscriptions, and book lists and orders.

Chapter 9. Socratic Questioning

1. Fabry, *The Pursuit of Meaning*, 155.
2. Lukas, *Meaningful Living*.
3. Ibid., 136.
4. Lawrence LeShan, *You Can Fight for Your Life* (New York: M. Evans and Co., Inc., 1980), 140.
5. Ibid.
6. Welter, *Connecting with a Friend*, 20–21.
7. Fabry, *The Pursuit of Meaning*, 5.
8. James D. Yoder, "Conscience in Logotherapeutic Counseling," *The International Forum for Logotherapy*, Vol. 8, No. 2 (Fall/Winter 1985), 104.
9. Ibid.
10. Ibid., 106.
11. Ibid.

Chapter 10. Paradoxical Intention

1. Lukas, *Meaningful Living*, 76.
2. Frankl, *Man's Search for Meaning*, 196–7.
3. Ibid., 199–200.
4. Lukas, *Meaningful Living*, 89.
5. Lukas, *Meaning in Suffering*, 46–47.
6. Lukas, *Meaningful Living*, 76–77.
7. Ibid., 77–78.
8. Frankl, *Man's Search for Meaning*, 196–7.
9. Lukas, "The 'Birthmarks' of Paradoxical Intention," *The International Forum for Logotherapy*, Vol. 5, No. 1 (Spring/Summer 1982), 20.
10. Edith Weisskopf-Joelson, "Some Comments on a Viennese School of Psychiatry," *The Journal of Abnormal and Social Psychology* 51 (1955) 701–3.
11. Frankl, *Man's Search for Meaning*, 203.
12. Lukas, "The 'Birthmarks' of Paradoxical Intention," 23.
13. Ibid.
14. Ibid., 24.
15. Joseph B. Fabry, Reuven P. Bulka, and William S. Sahakian (eds.), *Logotherapy in Action* (New York: Jason Aronson, 1979).
16. Ibid., 126.

17. James D. Yoder, "A Child, Paradoxical Intention, and Consciousness," *The International Forum for Logotherapy*, Vol. 6, No. 1 (Spring/Summer 1983), 19–21.

18. Ibid., 21.

19. Ibid.

20. Ibid.

21. Fabry, et al, *Logotherapy in Action*, 125.

Chapter 11. Dereflection

1. Quoted by Walter G. Oleksy in *The Power of Concentration* (Allen, Tex.: Argus Communications, 1981), 1.

2. Fabry, *The Pursuit of Meaning*, 142.

3. Ibid.

4. Lukas, *Meaningful Living*, 91–92.

5. Lukas, *Meaning in Suffering*, 152.

Chapter 12. Loss, Grief, and Emptiness

1. Paul Tournier, *To Understand Each Other* (Atlanta: John Knox Press, 1967), 50.

2. Quoted in Nathan A. Scott (ed.), *The Modern Vision of Death* (Richmond: John Knox Press, 1967), 11.

Chapter 13. Intervention with Cancer Patients

1. LeShan, *You Can Fight for Your Life*.

2. Ibid., 71–72.

3. Ibid., 111.

4. Ibid., 93.

5. Ibid., 99.

6. Ibid., 116.

7. Ibid.

8. Ibid., 143.

9. Irvin Yalom, "The 'Terrestrial' Meanings of Life, *The International Forum for Logotherapy*, Vol. 5, No. 2 (Fall/Winter 1982), 93.

10. Ibid.

Chapter 14. Counseling the Depressed Person for Meaning

1. Frankl, *The Unconscious God*, 96.
2. Lukas, *Meaningful Living*, 116.
3. Frankl, *The Unheard Cry for Meaning*.
4. Archibald Hart, *Adrenalin & Stress* (Waco, Tex.: Word Books, 1986), 149.
5. Ibid.
6. Ibid., 152.
7. C. S. Lewis, *Essays Presented to Charles Williams* (Grand Rapids, Mich.: William B. Eerdmans Pub. Co., 1947, 1966), xii.
8. Ibid., xii–xiii.
9. Weisskopf-Joelson, "Some Comments on a Viennese School of Psychiatry," 701–3.
10. Ibid.
11. Ibid.
12. The test catalog describing the tests and giving prices is available from Psychometric Affiliates, P. O. Box 3167, Munster, IN 46321. Those who request information and order tests need to use institutional stationery and note their qualifications as counselors.
13. Available from the same source in note 12, above.

Chapter 15. Violence and Meaning

1. Rollo May, *Power and Innocence* (New York: W. W. Norton & Co., Inc., 1972), 23.
2. Frankl, *The Unconscious God*, 96–97.
3. May, *Power and Innocence*, 24.
4. May, *The Courage to Create* (New York: Bantam Books, 1975).
5. Ibid., 3.
6. Paul Tournier, *The Violence Within* (San Francisco: Harper & Row, 1978).
7. Ibid., 11–12. Tournier quoted here from Georges Gusdorf's book, *La vertu de force* (Paris: Presses universitaires de France, 1957).
8. Ibid., 45.
9. Daniel Jay Sonkin and Michael Durphy, *Learning to Live without Violence* (San Francisco: Volcano Press, 1985), 13.
10. Ibid.
11. Ibid., 2.
12. Ibid.
13. Tournier, *The Violence Within*, 123.

14. Earnest Larsen, *Treat Me Easy* (Liguori, Mo.: Liguori Publications, 1975), 86, 87.

15. Drummond, *The Greatest Thing in the World*, 50–51.

16. Some of the material on gentleness in this chapter is from my column on "Marriage and the Family," *Faith at Work* (July/August 1979), 32. Used by permission.

Chapter 16. Addiction and Meaning

1. Lukas, *Meaning in Suffering*, 114.

2. William James, *Varieties of Religious Experience*, quoted in Fabry, et al, *Logotherapy in Action*, 244.

3. Ibid., 250.

4. James Crumbaugh, "Logotherapy: New Help for Problem Drinkers," *The International Forum for Logotherapy*, Vol. 4, No. 1 (Spring/Summer 1981).

5. Ibid., 31–34.

6. Anne Wilson Schaef, *Co-Dependence: Misunderstood—Mistreated* (Minneapolis: Winston Press, Inc., 1986), 21.

7. Ibid., 64–65.

Chapter 17. Guilt, Grace, and Meaning

1. William D. Eisenhower, "Fearing God," *Christianity Today* (Feb. 7, 1986), 33.

2. Ibid.

3. Paul Tournier, *Guilt and Grace* (New York: Harper & Row, 1958), 152.

4. Tournier, *Guilt and Grace*, 203.

5. Tweedie, *Logotherapy and the Christian Faith*, 168.

6. Lukas, *Meaning in Suffering*, 81–94.

7. Tweedie, *Logotherapy and the Christian Faith*, 179.

8. Michel Quoist, *Prayers* (New York: Avon Books, 1963), 137.

9. W. E. Vine, *An Expository Dictionary of New Testament Words*, (Old Tappan, N.J.: Fleming H. Revell Co., 1940), 170.

10. Henri J. M. Nouwen, *With Open Hands* (New York: Ballantine Books, 1972), 8.

Chapter 18. Suffering—Pain or Misery?

1. Useful resources for counselors who want to learn more about the family systems approach include Salvador Minuchin's books,

Family Therapy Techniques (1981, with Charles Fishman), and *Family Kaleidoscope* (1984), both Harvard University Press books, Cambridge, Mass.; also Virginia Satir's *Conjoint Family Therapy* (Palo Alto, Calif.: Science and Behavior Books, 1983, 3rd ed.).

2. Patricia L. Starck, "Patients' Perception of the Meaning of Suffering," *The International Forum for Logotherapy,* Vol. 6, No. 2 (Fall/Winter 1983), 110–16.

3. Ibid., 113.

4. Frankl, *The Doctor and the Soul,* 113.

5. Carl E. Braaten, *The Apostolic Imperative* (Minneapolis: Augsburg, 1985), 28.

Chapter 19. Counseling Children for Meaning

1. Bruno Bettelheim, *The Uses of Enchantment* (New York: Vintage Books, 1977), 3.

2. Ibid., 4.

3. Ibid., 145.

4. Paul Lewis, *Forty Ways to Teach Your Child Values* (Wheaton, Ill.: Tyndale House Publishers, Inc., 1985).

5. Subscription information for *Dad's Only* available from P. O. Box 340, Julian, CA 92036.

6. "New Ways to Talk About Children," *Varsity Educator,* Vol. 1, No. 3 (Aug./Sept. 1986). The source of this newsletter is SRI Perceiver Academies, Inc., P. O. Box 5700, Lincoln, NE 68505.

7. Ibid.

8. Pascal.

Chapter 20. Counseling Youth for Meaning

1. Richard Nelson Bolles, *The Three Boxes of Life: And How to Get Out of Them* (Berkeley: Ten Speed Press, 1981), 18.

2. Ibid., 46.

3. Quoted by Tony Compolo in "Just an Ordinary Hero," an article written by Kathleen Corcoran in *Inter-Varsity* (Summer 1986), 5.

4. Stephen S. Kalmar, "What Logotherapy Can Learn from High School Students," *The International Forum for Logotherapy,* Vol. 5, No. 2 (Fall/Winter 1982), 77–84.

5. Ibid., 78.

Chapter 21. Meaning as a Resource in Marriage Counseling

1. Quoted by Henri J. M. Nouwen, *The Living Reminder* (New York: Seabury Press, 1981), 66. The quote is from Elie Wiesel, *The Gates of the Forest* (New York: Holt, Rinehart, and Winston, 1966).
2. Murray Bowen, *Family Therapy in Clinical Practice* (New York: Jason Aronson, 1978).
3. Ibid., 491.
4. One such resource is a thirty-one-minute videotape, "Constructing the Multigenerational Family Genogram: Exploring a Problem in Context." The rental and/or purchase price for this and other resources may be obtained by writing Dept. 2, Menninger Video Productions, The Menninger Foundation, Box 829, Topeka, KS 66601 or by calling 800-345-6036.

A comprehensive treatment of genograms may be found in the book *Genograms in Family Assessment,* by Monica McGoldrick and Randy Gerson (New York: W. W. Norton and Co., 1985). This book uses genograms to depict the stories of a number of famous families, such as the Freuds, Roosevelts, and Kennedys. The reader is thus provided with real illustrations which help in learning to construct genograms.
5. Charlie Shedd and Martha Shedd, *Celebration in the Bedroom* (Waco, Tex.: Word Books, 1981).
6. Bolles, *The Three Boxes of Life.*
7. John Steinbeck, *Travels with Charlie* (New York: Viking Press, 1962).
8. Ibid., 4.
9. Bill Coleman, *It's Been a Good Year: The Anniversary Book* (Minneapolis: Bethany House Publishers, 1986).

Chapter 22. Finding Meaning in the Workplace

1. Richard Nelson Bolles, *The Three Boxes of Life: And How to Get Out of Them* (Berkeley: Ten Speed Press, 1981).
2. Bolles, *What Color Is Your Parachute?* (Berkeley: Ten Speed Press, 1986). This book is updated yearly.
3. Bolles, *The Three Boxes of Life,* 14.

Chapter 23. Counseling the Retired and Elderly for Meaning

1. Steinbeck, *Travels with Charlie.*
2. Ibid., 243.

3. Ibid.
4. Ibid.
5. LeShan, "Fighting for your Life: Stress, Cancer and Family Health," an audio cassette tape of a speech Dr. LeShan gave during the "Building Family Strengths Conference," at the University of Nebraska, Lincoln (May, 1984).
6. This work is described in detail in Paul Welter, "Training Retirement Center and Nursing Home Staff and Residents in Helping and Counseling Skills," *Journal of Psychology and Christianity*, Vol. 6 (1987), 2.
7. Paul Welter, *The Nursing Home: A Caring Community* (Valley Forge, Penn.: Judson Press, 1981).
8. Carolyn B. Stevens, *Special Needs of Long-Term Patients* (Philadelphia: J. B. Lippincott Co., 1974), 1.
9. Bruce Bliven, as quoted in Ruth Weinstock, *The Graying of the Campus* (New York: Educational Facilities Laboratory, 1978), 45.
10. Gail Sheehy, *Pathfinders* (New York: Bantam Books, 1981).
11. Ibid., 15.
12. Ibid.

Chapter 24. Self-Esteem and Meaning

1. Dag Hammarskjöld, *Markings* (New York: Knopf, 1964), 174.
2. Kelsey, *Caring*, 61.
3. May, *Man's Search for Himself*, 98–99.
4. Frankl, *Man's Search for Meaning*, 176.
5. J. R. R. Tolkien, *The Hobbit* (New York: Ballantine Books, 1973). *Lord of the Rings* (Boston: Houghton-Mifflin Co., 2nd ed., 1967).
6. Humphrey Carpenter (ed.), *The Letters of J. R. R. Tolkien* (Boston: Houghton-Mifflin Co., 1981).
7. Ibid., 149.
8. May, *Man's Search for Himself*, 224.

Chapter 25. Helping Clients Become Responsible

1. Frankl, *Man's Search for Meaning*, 167.
2. John Naisbitt, *Megatrends* (New York: Warner Books, 1984).
3. Many communities have STEP programs on a continuing basis

for parents. In between the nine weekly sessions parents apply their new-found skills with their children. Consult your human service directory or call your community continuing education office for information on parenting programs. The STEP program is marketed through American Guidance Services Publishers' Building, P. O. Box 99, Circle Pines, Minn. 55014–1796.

4. Don Dinkmeyer and Gary D. McKay, *The Parent's Handbook* (Circle Pines, Minn.: American Guidance Service, 1982).

Chapter 26. Evil as a Cause of Meaninglessness and Confusion

1. Kelsey, *Caring*, 175.
2. Peck, *People of the Lie*, 137.
3. Bruno Bettelheim, *The Uses of Enchantment*, 7.
4. Peck, *People of the Lie*, 207.
5. Ibid., 206.
6. Kelsey, *Caring*, 19.
7. Rudyard Kipling, *Something of Myself for My Friends Known and Unknown* (Garden City, N.Y.: Doubleday Doran & Co., 1937), 17.

Chapter 27. Finding Meaning through Creating

1. Van Andics, *Suicide and the Meaning of Life* (London: William Hodge, 1947), 178. Quoted in Yalom, "The 'Terrestrial' Meanings of Life," 9.
2. Teresa Amabile, "The Personality of Creativity," *Brandeis Review*, Vol. 5, No. 1 (Fall 1985), 7.
3. Ibid., 8.
4. May, *The Courage to Create*, 19.
5. Ashley Montagu, *Growing Young* (New York: McGraw-Hill Book Co., 1981), 157.
6. Paul Welter, *Learning from Children* (Wheaton, IL: Tyndale House Publishers, Inc., 1984), 128–9.
7. Ronald Gross, ed., *Invitation to Lifelong Learning* (Chicago: Follett Publishing Co., 1982). The Walt Whitman quote is by Eduard C. Lindeman, "To Put Meaning into the Whole of Life," 121.
8. Ibid.
9. The SDLP is described in the Introduction of this book. The creator of the SDLP, Malcolm Knowles, has an important article on

lifelong learning in the Gross book mentioned above: "Andragogy: The New Science of Education," 144–51.

Chapter 28. Humor—A Tool to Use in the Discovery of Meaning

1. Fabry, *The Pursuit of Meaning*, 134.
2. Information regarding the price of subscriptions and old issues may be obtained from The Humor Project, 110 Spring St., Saratoga Springs, N.Y. 12866.
3. Hiroshi Takashima, *Humanistic Psychosomatic Medicine* (Berkeley: Institute of Logotherapy Press, 1984).
4. Ibid., 55.
5. Ibid.
6. Michael F. Shaughnessy, "Humor in Logotherapy," *The International Forum for Logotherapy*, Vol. 7, No. 2 (Fall/Winter 1984), 108. This is an excellent article on the use of humor in counseling.

Chapter 29. The Meaning of the Moment

1. May, *The Discovery of Being*, 141.
2. Ibid.
3. Ibid., 156.

Chapter 30. Introducing Clients to Intergenerational Resources

1. Dennis C. Benson and Stan J. Stewart, *The Ministry of the Child* (Nashville: Abingdon, 1978, 1979).
2. Ibid., 12.

Chapter 31. The Meaning of Touch

1. Ashley Montagu, *Touching* (New York: Harper & Row, 1986), xiv.
2. Ibid., xiii.
3. Brown, *The Many Facets of Touch*, 185.
4. Montagu, *Touching*, 3.

5. Hermann Hesse, *Siddhartha* (New York: New Direction Pub. Co., 1951).

6. Ibid., 119.

7. Ibid., 122.

8. Jules Older, *Touching Is Healing* (New York: Stein and Day, 1982), 216–7. This book is a breath of fresh air. In it Older records his learnings about touch from his travels around the world. His thirty-three-page annotated bibliography on touch is superb. He calls it an "Opinionated Bibliography." His opinions regarding the various entries range from "a breath-taking success," to "nasty, brutish, and short-sighted," to "take with a half-gram of sodium chloride."

9. Montagu, *Touching*, 280.

10. Ibid.

11. Ibid., 360.

12. Older, *Touching Is Healing*, 200–201.

13. Montagu, *Touching*, 222.

14. Older, *Touching Is Healing*, 217.

Chapter 32. Terminating Counseling—The Meaning of Leaving

1. Nouwen, *The Living Reminder*, 45.

2. John Bowlby, *Separation: Anxiety and Anger* (New York: Basic Books, 1973), 253.

3. Nouwen, *The Living Reminder*, 47.

4. Ibid., 45.

PART III. The Counselor's Use of Self

1. Arthur Combs, *Helping Relationships* (Boston: Allyn and Bacon, Inc., 1971).

2. Ibid., 5.

3. Ibid.

4. May, *The Discovery of Being*, 156.

Chapter 33. Receiving from Clients

1. Kelsey, *Caring*, 82.

Chapter 34. The Pastor's Two Families

1. Kelsey, *Caring*, 85.

Chapter 35. Joining Your Client

1. "Perhaps Love," Placido Domingo with John Denver. CBS Stereo Cassette, Manufactured by CBS Records, CBS, Inc., N.Y., 1981.
2. Lukas, "The Best Possible Advice," *The International Forum for Logotherapy*, Vol. 3, No. 2 (Fall 1980), 14.
3. May, *The Discovery of Being*, 10.
4. Welter, *Connecting with a Friend*.

Chapter 36. The Wind from Heaven

1. Viktor Frankl, "Psychotherapy on Its Way to Rehumanism," *The International Forum for Logotherapy*, Vol. 3, No. 2 (Fall 1980), 6.
2. Pascal, *Thoughts, Letters, and Minor Works*.
3. Ibid., 96.
4. Nouwen, *The Living Reminder*, 33.

Chapter 37. Meaning, Justice, and Service

1. Braaten, *The Apostolic Imperative*, 7.
2. William E. Pannell, "Conversion: Expectations and Responsibilities," *Theology News and Notes*, Vol. XXXIII, No. 2 (Fuller Theological Seminary, June 1986), 22.
3. Ibid., 23.
4. Roger Fredrikson, *God Loves the Dandelions* (Waco, Tex.: Word Books, 1975).

Chapter 38. Meaning and Health

1. Quoted by Carl E. Thoresen and Jean R. Eagleston, "Counseling for Health," *The Counseling Psychologist*, Vol. 13, No. 1 (January 1985), 78.

2. Ibid. This is a substantive article on this subject. It is the major contribution to this issue, is seventy-two pages long, and includes eight pages of references related to counseling and health.

3. Ibid., 25.

4. Ibid., 26.

5. Ibid.

6. Ibid., 45.

7. Charles E. Hummel, "Tyranny of the Urgent" (a booklet published by Inter-Varsity Press, Downers Grove, Ill., 1967), p.4.

8. LeShan, *You Can Fight for Your Life*.

9. Ibid., 182.

Chapter 39. Training Listener-Responders in Churches

1. Kelsey, *Caring*, 79.

2. Gary Collins, *Innovative Approaches to Counseling*, Resources for Christian Counseling Vol. 1 (Waco, Tex.: Word Books, 1986), 195–6.

3. Welter, *Connecting with a Friend*.

4. Mignon Eisenberg, "Rehumanizing University Teaching," *The International Forum for Logotherapy*, Vol. 8, No. 1 (Spring/Summer 1985), 44–46.

5. Arthur T. Jersild, *When Teachers Face Themselves* (New York: Teachers College, Columbia University, 1955), 84.

6. Paul Ford, "C. S. Lewis: Soul Friend," *Theology News and Notes* (Fuller Theological Seminary, October 1982), 17.

7. Faith at Work, 11065 Little Patuxent Parkway, Columbia, MD 21044.

8. Director of Training, Institute of Logotherapy, P. O. Box 156, Berkeley, CA 94704.

INDEX

259